Trends in Language Teaching

Trends in Language Teaching

Edited by

Rama Kant Agnihotri

Anju Sahgal Gupta

A. L. Khanna

Orient BlackSwan

The publisher and authors are grateful to the Commissioner, School Education, West Bengal for permission to include the illustration from *Kishalay*-II originally published (1982) by the West Bengal Board of Primary Education, on page 88 of this book.

TRENDS IN LANGUAGE TEACHING

ORIENT BLACKSWAN PRIVATE LIMITED

Registered Office
3-6-752 Himayatnagar, Hyderabad 500 029 (Telangana), INDIA
e-mail: centraloffice@orientblackswan.com

Other Offices
Bengaluru, Bhopal, Chennai, Guwahati, Hyderabad, Jaipur, Kolkata, Lucknow, Mumbai, New Delhi, Noida, Patna, Vijayawada

First Published 2017

ISBN 978-93-86296-87-0

025029
25012017

Typeset in
Bembo Std 11/13
by Manmohan Kumar, Delhi

Printed in India at
B. B. Press
Noida

Published by
Orient Blackswan Private Limited
3-6-752 Himayatnagar
e-mail: info@orientblackswan.com

The illustrations on pages 72 and 93 are representative samples of the original versions.
Illustrator: Sayan Chakraborty

Contents

List of Figures and Tables

Figures

Tables

CHAPTER 1

Introduction

The approaches to language learning and teaching are changing very rapidly and traditional ways are increasingly being influenced by new research and insights in how we learn languages. Many of our old teacher-centred approaches are considered obsolete and there is an increasing awareness about diversity, advantages of multilingualism and the developments in the areas of internet and other forms of technology. The focus is no longer on memorisation and rote learning, or even on language as a mere form of communication but on using language and cultural knowledge as a foundation for encoding systems of knowledge and connecting with local identities on the one hand and the global community on the other. Today language teaching is more learner-centred, collaborative, and often technology driven. It is rapidly moving towards empowering the learner by reposing faith in the linguistic and cultural resources she comes with in the classroom and by making the teacher aware of classroom diversities and new techniques of teaching. Learners, their linguistic and cultural resources, needs, hopes and aspirations are kept at the heart of language learning and education. There is a recognition and celebration of diversity and differences, valuing greater learner participation in the creation of knowledge, exploring the fuzzy and the unclear rather than focusing only on the known and established ways of doing things. The languages and cultural practices children bring with them to school are slowly beginning to receive greater attention and be treated as an asset rather than an obstacle. Multilingualism available as a default condition in the classrooms is seen as a resource, a basis for pedagogical strategy and a goal to be nourished as it correlates positively with cognitive growth, scholastic achievement, language proficiency, metalinguistic awareness and social tolerance. Three most distinguishing features of the contemporary trends in language teaching are learner-centredness, reorientation of teacher education and recognition of linguistic and cultural diversity seen in any classroom. Though all this may not hold true everywhere in India as yet, it appears to be the way forward. That's why we think this book is timely.

Learner Centredness

Student-centred approaches are definitely the focus, as is recognising the need for learner autonomy and cooperative learning (Jacobs and Farrell 2001 in Eaton 2010). In the twenty-first century, individualised instruction is becoming the norm. As educators and schools recognise and celebrate students' demonstrations of knowledge in clear and tangible ways, so too are we celebrating students' individual talents, aptitudes and skills. Not only is learning becoming more student-centred, but also student participation in the development of outcomes for learning is on the rise. (Pauk 2007 in Eaton 2010).

There is a movement towards learning other languages as a means not only to become self-empowered, but also to empower others. Learning a language in order to reach out to others and make a difference in the world is becoming common. Old, authoritarian models are giving way to gentler and more collaborative models. Today's language classroom is vastly different from that of the mid- to late twentieth century. The focus is no longer on grammar, memorisation and learning by rote, but rather using language and cultural knowledge as a means to connect to others around the globe. Geographical and physical boundaries are being transcended by technology as students learn to reach out to the world around them, using their language and cultural skills to facilitate the connections they are eager to make.

Linguistic and Cultural Diversity

It is now explicitly recognised by policy makers, practitioners and professional experts that classrooms and schools are characterised by a diversity of linguistic and cultural practices. As the National Curriculum Framework (NCF, 2005) and the Position Papers on the Teaching of Indian Languages (NCERT, 2005a) and the Teaching of English (NCERT, 2005b) claim, languages available in the classroom can be used as a resource rather than an obstacle in pedagogical practices. For a whole range of studies on pedagogical practices rooted in multilingualism see Achmat (1992), Agnihotri (1995, 2006, 2007, 2009, 2010, 2014), García (2009), Heugh (2010) among others. All these studies demonstrate the intense relationship that obtains between the language of the child and her social and cognitive development and show how these languages can be used as a resource to achieve proficiency in the target languages, enhancing metalinguistic awareness, cognitive growth, scholastic achievement and social tolerance. It is necessary for the teachers and teacher educators to have a theoretical and practical base for creating language classrooms that meet the needs of linguistically and culturally diverse learners.

Teachers also need to be sensitive to the variety of ways in which children are denigrated and put into categories such as 'girls', 'backward', 'from denotified tribe', *dehati* ('rural'), *ganvaru* ('idiot') or 'disabled'. It is of utmost importance that teachers and teacher educators realise that *all* normal children (i.e. except those who are born with major cognitive deficits) are born with a Language Faculty and are equally equipped to learn different languages and various systems of knowledge. For example, there is no reason why a hearing-impaired child may not be able to learn everything using Sign Language or a visually impaired child may not be in a position to learn all subjects using a software like Jaws.

Teachers and Teacher Educators

In recent years, educators have become more aware of the need to re-evaluate their teaching practices to deal with not just different languages, but also different abilities, knowledge bases, motivation and interests of both children and teachers. Teachers need to plan their lessons keeping this differentiation in mind in order to accommodate diversity in the classroom.

Teachers

- must respect all learners as individuals with distinct culturally defined identities;
- should recognise that learners bring funds of knowledge to their learning communities and must incorporate this knowledge and experience into their classroom practice;
- should accept that learners have a right to a variety of educational experiences that help them make informed decisions about their role and participation in language, literacy, and life;
- need to model culturally responsive and socially responsible practices for learners;
- admit that learners need to be taught mainstream power codes/discourses while also having their home and street codes recognised and respected; and
- need to be advocates for and models of social justice and equity.

Language teachers

In recent years, the conceptualisation and practice of education of language teachers has undergone a significant change. It has travelled far beyond merely an introduction to the history of language teaching and an understanding of the methods, materials and assessment procedures used in the classrooms. It has now become increasingly important to introduce teachers to the nature and structure of language, and its acquisition and change. It is very important to familiarise teachers with different varieties of a human language and to empower them to use the multiplicity of linguistic and cultural practices available in the classrooms as resources for linguistic and cognitive growth of the learners. There is also a need to sensitise them to the specific needs of the underprivileged children. An awareness about the different ways in which teachers can help eliminate gender discrimination in the class and arrange suitable facilities for children with disabilities to learn different languages is indeed a major challenge. Above all, a teacher should understand that a meaningful language activity will not just consist of children individually or in groups performing some routine tasks; it needs to be pitched at a level slightly higher than the existing cognitive levels of children (that is what Krashen 1985 calls 'i + 1'), and should make them reflect over what they are doing and present challenging scenarios in front of them to respond to.

Beyond Method

For over a century, 'language educators sought to solve the problems of language teaching by focusing attention almost exclusively on Method' (Stern 1983: 452). Traditionally it was believed that if we followed the right set of teaching principles it would lead to the most effective learning outcomes. However, this thinking has been questioned in recent times as we have witnessed the rise and fall of several methods throughout the recent history of language teaching learning (Brown 2002). Hence, now there is disillusionment with 'methods' as a problem solver for the teaching learning problem. In this 'post methods era', attention has shifted from **method** to **pedagogy**, i.e. to the teaching learning processes and the contribution of the teacher to this process.

To quote, Kumaravadivelu (2006):

> We have been awakened to the necessity of making methods-based pedagogies more sensitive to local exigencies, awakened to the opportunity afforded by post method pedagogies to help practicing teachers develop their own theory of practice, awakened to the multiplicity of learner identities, awakened to the complexity of teacher beliefs, and awakened to the vitality of macrostructures—social, cultural, political, and historical—that shape and reshape the microstructures of our pedagogic enterprise. (p. 75)

There is a need to create language teaching modules that are sensitive to the languages of children, their socio-cultural background and their differential skills and abilities. We have been in the past using procedures such as dictation, translation and précis writing in a rather thoughtless and ruthless fashion. Today, we know that these can be used as integrative and challenging language teaching procedures which would engage learners creatively and challenge and enhance their linguistic and cognitive abilities. There is now an academic and research consensus that supports the use of translation and L1 in the language classroom. A return to translation techniques does not, however, mean that we should return to the dry and dusty days of the past. There are a range of new, lively and communicative classroom activities that involve translation. We also have a substantial number of pedagogical practices that are rooted in the languages of children and take them through the processes of data collection, classification and categorisation, pattern analysis, rule formation and hypothesis testing (see for example Achmat 1992; Agnihotri 1995, 2007, 2009, 2010, 2014; Mohanty et al 2009; Heugh 2010 among others).

Anandan (2012) in his interview talks about 'discourse oriented pedagogy' for teaching of English that he evolved over a period of time after trying out several models of teaching. He contends that this pedagogic model is built on the claim that a language cannot be acquired by simply learning the elements of the language, and practising language skills. He points out, 'Since language exists only as meaningful discourses, both the input and output should be in the form of discourses. Textbooks need not merely have slots for practising language elements and vocabulary. Instead, they should contain discourse tasks which take care of both language elements and skills.'(p. 38)

Globalisation, ICT and Language Teaching

Let us first look at in some detail on globalisation and its impact on language teaching. In an economy based on services and information, the linguistic skills of workers become increasingly important and language becomes an economic commodity with a value in the market place. New technologies make it possible to have new kinds of language teaching. This has implications for how and why people learn languages, and which languages they learn.

It has created a necessity for linguists as well as language teachers to fully understand the learner factors and their influence on the way first and second/foreign languages should now be taught. The fast-growing area of information technology has also contributed to restructuring language teaching policy in our country. The renewed focus on the language curricula of primary schools, revision of language teacher training curricula of education, and computer laboratories with internet access in schools are concrete indicators of the effect of information technology on language teaching in India.

Globalisation has led to the development and highly intensified use of Information and Communication Technology (ICT). Kim (2011) cites several research findings to justify this claim. According to McCrum R et al., (1986), mentioned in Kim (2011), the high growth of computer and the Internet use has made information, which is 80% written in English very easy to access. As a result of this revolution, many activities in the field of language use and teaching can be carried out quickly and accurately. The massive use of technology is manifested in web-based learning, emails, blogs, Skype, mobile telephones, iPods etc. Kim (2011) says:

> In web-based classes, students can easily ask for lessons or exercises which accord with their language level. Thousands of English web-based classes offer training for a variety of basic language skills (listening, speaking, writing, and reading). These skills can be put on the web and made interactive in a variety of ways, for example with Internet communication tools such as m-learning, email, blogs, chat. These tools provide integrated environment for teachers and students. Many web-based classes also facilitate the study of vocabulary, pronunciation and other branches of language learning. This is made possible by ICT that can hold and present vast amounts of real language data in a compact audio-visual. (p. 10)

Kim (2011) points out how email can be fruitfully used by teachers to provide feedback to the work done by the students. Blogging becomes communicative and interactive when participants assume multiple roles in the writing process, as writers who write and post, as readers/reviewers who respond to other writers' posts, and as writer-readers who, returning to their own posts, react to criticism of their own posts. Readers in turn can comment on what they read. Using Skype, students can develop their speaking skill and improve their pronunciation. They can interact with other speakers of English who are speaking different varieties of English and compare their own speech with theirs. iPods provide a variety of possibilities for language learners to enhance their listening, pronunciation, vocabulary, grammar and writing. For instance, teachers can send text messages and students read and answer the message. Students also can record their voices so that they can do listening and speaking exercises at the same time.

According to Miranda and Francis (2010), 'the escalating use of mobile telephones has even overtaken the growth rate of internet access among the people in India. According to Telecom Regulatory Authority of India (TRAI) data, India had 635.51 million mobile phone users at the end of June 2010, projecting phenomenal growth in teledensity. Today India is the second-largest wireless market in the world after China' (p. 16). Kurup and Tripathy (2010) predict that India's mobile subscriber base will grow to 993 million by 2014. Learning at one's pace has become possible through these devices like cellular phones enabling learners to collaborate, create, and evaluate their own learning processes. The primary advantage of the mobile device is that information stored in it can be used anytime, anywhere. Another advantage is that the mobile device is cheaper than computers and laptops, hence majority of the learners can afford and benefit from it. It does not need continuous supply of electricity that makes it easier to use, especially in rural areas where there is intermittent electricity. It is a more light-weight device compared to computers and books and easy to carry (Miranda 2012).

With Evernote (a cloud-based note-taking and file storage application), students can have digital notebooks for all subject areas which can include all kinds of virtual files. Evernote can also be synched with Twitter for student-teacher blogging and sharing. Students can finally have the chance to spend less time on routine tasks and more time on actual learning by using Evernote. Evernote can automatically sync a student's account to any technological device, such as iPhones, iPads, BlackBerrys, Androids etc. Students will literally have access to their yearly college portfolio in their pocket. The best thing is that Evernote lasts a lifetime. Rather than saving documents and notebooks, everyone can go paperless with Evernote.

Wikispaces allows students to obtain instantaneous information regarding class assignments and announcements from anywhere inside or outside the classroom; it enables them to download course documents they missed or lost, gives teachers a forum where they can pass on last-minute announcements, and allows students a place to keep their e-portfolio entries. It also permits the teacher to track students' submitted entries.

Technology is used not for the sake of technology. It is used for sharing the knowledge of the students to help them create their own projects. Eaton (2010) points out,

> In addition to the technologies that demonstrate student learning, there are also the technologies that facilitate student learning. These technologies may be synchronous (done in real time), such as Skype, Moodle or virtual live classes; or they may be asynchronous (not done in real time) such as podcasts and blogs. It is likely that asynchronous technology will give way to synchronous technologies as the latter become more effective. Let's take it one step further: mobile technology for earning is definitely in. It's called 'MALL' (Mobile Assisted Language Learning) and it is quickly gaining as much buzz today as 'CALL' (Computer Assisted Language Learning) created in the 1980s and 90s (Chinnery, 2006; Collins, 2005; Kukulska-Hulme and Shield, 2007, 2008). It is not impossible that in the future 'apps' or some variation of mobile applications, may replace textbooks. Students are harnessing their creativity to express themselves and demonstrate what they know using technology. The challenge for the twenty-first century teacher will be to find ways to allow them to do that. In today's world, students are the creators, not simply consumers, of technology and technology-produced art and projects (p.14).

Assessment

Over the last two decades, there has been a worldwide movement towards the development and implementation of benchmark systems and frameworks that take an asset-based approach to language assessment. Traditional models of testing revealed 'gaps' in students' knowledge. There was an underlying expectation that if only these gaps could be filled with the appropriate knowledge, students' learning would be complete. This is now outdated. Educational leaders of the new millennium are asking questions such as, 'What *can* my students do?' and 'How do we help them grow from where they are now?' It means recognising students' abilities to understand, use and produce language in a variety of forms, for a variety of purposes. Tharu (2011) comments that our responsibility as teachers is to 'discover/ understand where our learners are initially and help them move forward.' Only hardened autocrats will fail to see the possibilities of collaboration (learner participation) here. In this frame, teaching and assessment become mutually dependent and supportive. On-the-way assessment yielding formatively usable information comes to be seen as a necessary aspect of pedagogy.(p. 30) He further points out that 'if we come to value assessment as support for teaching, we would naturally want to engage in it more, also more purposefully and comprehensively. This would not depend on the official weight for internal assessment being raised (by orders from above). More assessment in this mode will shift the emphasis away from conventional summative evaluation.'(p. 30)

Samuel (2011) stresses that assessment over time is also important because learning is a continuous, dynamic process and ongoing assessment provides teachers with regular feedback on students' performance and enables them to adjust their actions accordingly. She enumerates multiple methods of assessment such as interviews with students, group and pair work, and several paper and pencil tests that offer a more holistic picture of students' learning than time-bound tests. She remarks, 'To conclude, we can only exploit tests as opportunities for teaching and continued development of our learners' skills and language proficiency when assessment is carried out by knowledgeable teachers and assessors who involve students in meaningful dialogues and create an atmosphere of mutual trust. They draw on a variety of strategies to observe and document their students' performance over a period of time as students are engaged in authentic tasks and help students to become lifelong learners by enabling them to be critical assessors of their own work.'(p. 15)

Asset-based approaches using benchmarks and frameworks are the new trends in language learning evaluation and assessment. Student portfolios are gaining popularity at a rapid pace. They are collaborative efforts between a student and a teacher that provide clear demonstrations of a student's progress and achievements. Students are guided by their teachers to develop their own portfolios over time. Student portfolios contain demonstrations of their knowledge and authentic language use. More and more, electronic portfolios are being used. The beauty of the student portfolio is that the student owns it, not the teacher. Students carry their portfolios forward from grade to grade, taking responsibility for their learning as they go on. Portfolios are an excellent tool to teach learners how to self-monitor and evaluate, as well as providing them with provable demonstrations of their learning.

Articles in the Book

We have deliberately not divided the book into any overt sections because we feel that there is a kind of seamlessness between theory and practice, between skills and theory and between the so called 'disabled and abled' people. This seamlessness seems to be the main thrust of the twenty-first century where sharp divisions are being blurred and interconnectivity between various aspects of the teaching-learning process seems to be developing. On the other hand, there is an equally powerful movement to pay attention to the needs and aspirations of individual learners.

For instance, there is a rapid scaling up of people who migrate between countries, regions, rural and urban contexts. This has immense implications for linguistic diversity in society which in turn impacts educational institutions. Instead of looking for drastic solutions for this, the author in her paper 'Translation and multilingual education' argues that we may hark back to the grammar-translation method, albeit in a new way. She suggests that we need to recognise the language learning practices that students use in their daily life, where they draw upon the languages known by one another and use their cognitive faculties to interpret and translate meaning among each other. She suggests that we need to value students' skills in translation, and recognise the cognitive processes of interpreting which are essential to language development. 'Multilingual education,' according to her, 'is often discussed as if it is unusual, difficult to implement, and requiring new or modern pedagogies. However, these are misconceptions.'

The next paper 'Innovations in research and teaching in multilingual classrooms' discusses the theoretical developments in research that capture innovative teaching practices in multilingual classrooms. It reviews three generations of innovations (or lack of them) in multilingual classroom practices. The first generation of research in multilingual and multicultural classroom contexts grew out of the field of linguistic anthropology in North America; the second generation of studies, emerging from the early 1990s onwards, developed critical, interpretive approaches to the study of multilingual classroom interaction; and the third generation of studies are opening up new epistemological spaces interfacing with other fields of research, such as multimodality in classroom interaction or ethnography of language policy, while building on the robust foundation of the first and second generations of research.

'Teaching Hindi as a less commonly taught language' ties in very well with the questions of mobility of people between nations. This paper looks at the teaching of Hindi in the American context as a less commonly taught language. Though Hindi teaching programs in several schools have become a significant part of the teaching schedule, the whole enterprise appears to be devoid of several required and supportive aspects of language teaching such as serious research, developing teaching materials, and teaching methods. The author takes a close look at several aspects of Hindi teaching, its engagement with sustainable teaching methodology, the target audience, and the relevance of required innovative approaches.

'Linguistic and cultural diversity and language teaching—with a specific focus on the teaching of reading and writing' addresses issues of diversity and home-school transition within mainstream classrooms for marginalised learners. Recent research has highlighted that the first one or two years in school are extremely important for facilitating a successful transition from home to school, especially for those young learners who are from diverse social, cultural and linguistic backgrounds and are actively encountering print for the first time when they enter school. Further, the Emergent Literacy perspective has emphasised that unless children acquire literate behaviours through using print and interacting with others within their social environments, they are often unable to go beyond a mechanical and incomplete mastery of the written code. This paper will present the field-based experience and insights arrived over the past six years through work undertaken within the Early Literacy Project (ELP). The conceptualisations of early literacy in the ELP intervention have been viewed within an overarching theoretical framework which positions itself within socio-cultural and constructivist perspectives, which privilege meaning over mechanical skills.

'Teaching language and achieving literacy: Interfering with learning, or guiding it?' uses anecdotal evidence to show that learning at school which is bereft of natural ways in which children develop language and literary skill, hinders language learning within the school system. The paper appeals for a synergy between teaching and cognitive science to inform the process of teacher formation in society.

There is plenty of research evidence to show that in real life children do not compartmentalise learning. In fact learning sometimes progresses from simpler, concrete, general and more holistic forms initially, to more complex, abstract, specific and fragmented learning at a later advanced stage; sometimes an understanding of the whole is acquired first and slowly the complexities are unfolded. This has great relevance to the development of reading and writing skills in the initial years of school. This essentially means that language learning is not confined to the area of the language class alone. Much of the language skills that develop at school are within other subject areas.

'Speaking of food: apple...ice-cream...posto...pesta...roti...' straddles subjects as diverse as language—literature, geography, history, mathematics and science. This paper sketches the continuum between the subjective and the historical contexts of food, with select examples from three language-literature textbooks, in Bangla, Hindi and English. Through these examples the author seeks to address the following questions: 'How can we create links between individual experience and multiple histories of learners to enrich classroom activities?', 'What kind of approaches would help teachers generate texts, exercises and projects?', 'In what ways would an inter-disciplinary approach enable the learner to express herself and discover ways of establishing a relationship with our rapidly changing environment?'

'General semantics, neuro-linguistic programming and language in the class-room' is a strand which is getting increasing popularity in the twenty-first century. The central tenet of Neuro-Linguistic Programming (NLP) may be said to lie in the statement 'The Map is not the Territory'. That is, the authors operate in this world on the basis of the map of the world and not the world itself. An awareness of the blocks, limitations, and distortions of the map can help us grow out of them and come closer to reality. The origin of the tenet goes back to General Semantics, founded by Alfred Korzybsky with the aim of developing scientific awareness about bringing language closer to reality, in order to avoid misevaluations and conflicts in the world of human interaction and to free ourselves from individual proclivities and biases. This paper shows how a concern with an understanding of the learner's map of the world, the teacher can help the learner overcome her limitations and offer her greater choices of growth.

These papers look at some of the theoretical issues which appear to be trending in this century where language teaching is concerned. There are also papers on the teaching of various skills.

In 'Reformulation as a technique for teaching writing' the authors assert that they are not advocating the notion of recasting sentences in order to correct errors in writing. Instead of pointing out errors, this technique aims at helping students complete the meaning of the sentence by using appropriate conventions of grammar (sentence level), cohesion and coherence (text level). It encourages students to produce another draft without reference to the original.

'Karaoke: A powerful tool to improve reading skills' shows how reading skills are improved when graphic and oral input is provided in an innovative and interesting way. A set of moving pictures with songs or other material accompanied by the words spoken, and written on the screen in the same language (Same Language Sub-

Titling), is used. The reading skills in English are improved by the use of karaoke. Songs were sung by the students as a group, with the words appearing on the moving strip.

The next paper 'The role of "noticing" in learning grammar' looks at how grammatical structures are internalised by the learner, specifically showing how procedural knowledge can be developed through form-focussed classroom tasks which encourage students to notice the rules of grammar.

'Exploring multiple intelligences through storytelling in the classroom' provides evidence to show that the well-known technique of story-telling continues to be a potent tool in the classroom even today and greatly so with young learners who emote with the character and the situation. The gains of storytelling range from language development, appreciation of literature, development of critical thinking skills, and an understanding of the community and self.

'Language teaching in inclusive education' questions the whole notion of disability and suggests that we are all able and disabled in different cultural and social contexts. The issues of making the world disabled-friendly arise ONLY because we have created a world keeping the idealised norm that hardly exists.

'Language teaching and learning for children with autism spectrum disorder' deals with inclusive education and talks about autism as a spectrum disorder with varying degree of severity and differences. It draws our attention to how children with mild to moderate impairments frequently find themselves in regular classroom, where they are expected to perform like their typically developing peers. When they are unable to cope, the difficulties are dismissed as bad behaviours. This paper attempts to outline the symptoms that indicate the presence of autism and help teachers to devise ways and means of helping these children integrate in the classroom setting.

Conclusion

There is a case for a reconceptualised field that is more learner-centred, more collaborative and more technologically driven and is more sensitive to the needs of the underprivileged and 'disabled' children. The trends in language learning are moving us towards empowering our students to communicate with others across the globe in real time. Diversity of the learners' characteristics, objectives, location, and culture and the accelerated changes that are rapidly taking place in the world community today make language teaching very complex and dynamic. The emergence and use of information and communication technology also helps us to face the challenges and offer new opportunities leading to innovations and best practices. Our present anthology of articles from various corners of the world aims at sharing some of these new trends and concerns in the contemporary classroom.

References

Achmat, (1992). The multilingual classroom video. http: //www.youtube. com/ watch?v=l74ULxuBM3E

Agnihotri, Rama Kant, (1995). 'Multilingualism as a classroom resource'. In K. Heugh, A. Sieruhn & P. Pluddemann (eds), *Multilingual Education for South Africa*. Johannesburg, Germany: Heinmann, 3–7.

——— (2006). 'Identity and multilinguality: The case of India'. In A. B. M. Tsui & J. W. Tollefson (eds), *Language Policy, Culture, and Identity in Asian Contexts*. Mahwah, NJ: Lawrence Erlbaum Associates, Inc, 185–204.

——— (2007). 'Towards a pedagogical paradigm rooted in multilinguality'. *International Multilingual Research Journal*, 1/ 2, 79–88.

——— (2009). 'Multilinguality and a new world order'. In A. K. Mohanty, M. Panda, R. Phillipson & T. Skutnabb-Kangas (eds), *Multilingual Education for Social Justice: Globalising the Local*. New Delhi: Orient BlackSwan, 268–77.

——— (2010). 'Multilinguality and the teaching of English in India'. *The EFL Journal*, 1/ 1, 1–14.

——— (2014). 'Multilinguality, education and harmony'. *International Journal of Multilingualism*, doi: 10.1080/14790718.2014.921181

Anandan, K. N., (2012). 'Face to face with K. N. Anandan'. *Language and Language Teaching*, 1/ 2, 37–39.

Chinnery, G. M., (2006). 'Emerging technologies: Going to the MALL (Mobile Assisted Language Learning)'. *Language Learning & Technology*, 10/ 1, 9–16.

Collins, T. G., (2005). 'English class on the air: Mobile language learning with cell phones'. Paper presented at the Fifth IEEE International Conference on Advanced Learning Technologies (ICALT'05).

Retrieved from http: // doi.ieeecomputersociety.org/10.1109/ICALT.2005.137

Eaton, S.E., (2010). *Global trends in language learning in the 21st century.* Calgary: Onate Press.

García, O., (2009). 'Education, multilingualism and translanguaging in the 21st century'. In A. K. Mohanty, M. Panda, R. Phillipson & T. Skutnabb-Kangas (eds), *Multilingual Education for Social Justice: Globalizing the Local.* New Delhi: Orient BlackSwan, 128–45.

Heugh, Kathleen, (2010). 'Productive engagement with linguistic diversity in tension with globalised discourses in Ethiopia'. *Current Issues in Language Planning,* 11/ 4, 378–96.

Jacobs, G. M., & T. S. C. Farrell, (2001). 'Paradigm shift: Understanding and implementing change in second language education'. *TESL-EJ.*

Retrieved May 15, 2010, from TESL-EJ: http: //tesl-ej.org/ej17/a1.html

Kim, Yong, (2011). 'Current trends in ELT'. *JET,* 1/1, February, 1–13.

Krashen, S.D., (1985). *The Input Hypothesis: Issues and Implications.* New York: Longman.

Kukulska-Hulme, A. & L. Shield, (2007). 'An overview of mobile assisted language learning: Can mobile devices support collaborative practices in speaking and listening?' Retrieved May 15 2010, from The Open University, UK: portal.acm.org/citation.cfm?id=1520087.

——— (2008). 'An overview of mobile assisted language learning: From content delivery to supported collaboration and interaction'. *ReCALL,* 20/3.

Kumaravadivelu, B., (2006). 'TESOL Methods: Changing tracks, challenging trends'. *TESOL Quarterly,* 40/1, March, 59–81.

Kurup, Rajesh & Devidutta Tripathy, (2010). 'Mobile users in India at 993 million in 2014: Researchers garter'. *Daily News and Analysis,* July 15 2010. Mumbai: Reuters. http: //www.dnaindia.com. Last accessed on 29 July 2010.

McCrum, R., W. Cran & R. McNeil, (1986). *The study of English.* London: Faber and Faber.

Miranda, Sapna & Roseliz Francis, (2010). 'Locating M-learning in India'. *FORTELL,* September, issue19, 16–17.

Miranda, Sapna (2012) 'm-Learning in India'. In A. L. Khanna and A. S. Gupta (ed.) *Essential Readings for Teachers of English: From Research Insights to Classroom Practices.* Delhi, Orient Blackswan.

Mohanty, A. K., M. Panda, R. Phillipson & T. Skutnabb-Kangas (eds), (2009). *Multilingual Education for Social Justice: Globalising the Local*. New Delhi: Orient Longman.

NCERT (2005). *National Curriculum Framework (NCF)*. New Delhi: National Council of Education Research and Training.

NCERT (2005a). 'Position paper on the teaching of Indian languages (NCF)'. New Delhi: National Council of Education Research and Training.

NCERT (2005b). 'Position paper on the teaching of English (NCF)'. New Delhi: National Council of Education Research and Training.

Pauk, B., (2007). 'Student participation in developing outcomes: A survey of students majoring in European Languages'. *Teaching and Learning Forum 2007*. Retrieved May 25, 2010, from http: //lsn.curtin.edu. au/tlf/tlf2007/refereed/pauk.html

Rea-Dickins, P., (2001). 'Mirror, mirror on the wall: Identifying processes of classroom assessment'. *Language Testing*, 18/4, 429–62.

Samuel, Nupur, (2011). 'Assessment: An opportunity to learn'. *FORTELL*, September 2011, issue 22, 12–15.

Tharu, Jacob, (2011). 'Beyond the achievement-proficiency divide: A new perspective on language assessment'. *FORTELL*, September 2011, issue 22, 28–30.

CHAPTER 2

Translation and Multilingual Education

KATHLEEN HEUGH

Abstract

Making use of the linguistic repertoires of students in the teaching of languages and subjects across the curriculum is not difficult and it is not dependent upon specialised and complex teacher development programmes. Multilingual education is often discussed as if it is unusual, difficult to implement, and requiring new or modern pedagogies. However, these are misconceptions. Good teaching simply requires teachers who focus on their students and how best to engage their students in learning. In most contexts of the world, this means navigating between the language repertoires which students use in their communities and one or more languages in which educational material is printed and in which school exit examinations are written. Navigating between languages or across linguistic divides involves cognitive language expertise in interpreting and translation. In this chapter, teachers of students in three different settings are shown to make use of translation, in order to use and build on what students know and in order to access and build expertise in the language of formal education. Translation, once a regular part of the old grammar-translation methodology has been diminished for several decades. However, its fundamental role in facilitating language development is once again being acknowledged in contemporary discussions of bilingual and multilingual education, although it is repackaged under a newly coined term 'translanguaging' (García 2009). In this chapter, translation is discussed as a valuable dimension to language education. It is something that good teachers recognise and use, and it is not regarded as new in India, South and South-East Asia or Africa. Even if 'translanguaging' is understood as a new pedagogical approach in language education in countries of the global north, the use of translation, which is integral to translanguaging, is not new, and it is available to every teacher.

Introduction

Developing strong language skills so that these can be used to navigate the academic curriculum applies to each level of the education system, whether this is in the primary, secondary, college or university classroom. While those of us who work in the so-called global south know that this inevitably means that we do this in multilingual contexts, others in the global north have thought that this was largely possible in one dominant language of socio-political and economic power. Recent trends which show a rapid scaling up of mobile people who migrate between countries, regions, rural and urban contexts, have implications for diversity. Current mobility has a significant impact on the scale of linguistic diversity in society, most particularly in educational institutions. Language teaching methodology and educational methodologies which intersect with linguistic diversity of this scale therefore encounter challenges which need innovative responses (Stroud & Heugh, 2011). While we often think of innovation as meaning something new, in this chapter, I argue that linguistic and cultural diversity do not need something new, rather we need to reclaim educational practices which we have ignored for much of the last four to five decades, and we need to recognise language learning practices that students use on a daily basis, but which have not yet been valued in the school setting. These are skills and expertise in translation and interpreting.

With the introduction of the 'direct method' followed by the 'communicative method' of teaching languages by Dell Hymes in the 1970s (see Hymes 1972 for example), we gave up the 'grammar-translation' method which was much stigmatised as too focussed on the form (structure) of language. It is quite true that the narrow focus on grammar and the structure of language was boring and ineffective as a mechanism for relevant language teaching, but it was unfortunate that translation was rejected along with grammar teaching. The focus here will be on reclaiming what is an essential part of the way that people learn languages in multilingual contexts, and that is by using their abilities to interpret spoken and translate written language. When we observe children playing in multilingual urban communities, we hear them making use of the languages known by one another. What they do is to use their cognitive faculties to interpret and translate meaning among each other. When we observe children in the school classroom, and we teach them in a language which is not one that they know well, we know that they have to rely on their ability to interpret and translate. However, in many parts of the world (perhaps all) we have stopped valuing students' skills in translation, and we have not yet recognised the cognitive processes of interpreting or the linguistic expertise upon which these rely and which are essential to language development.

I draw on three contexts to show the value of translation in language teaching and learning. These are: my involvement in a teacher education programme which was intended to prepare teachers in South Africa to develop their students' trilingualism in the late 1990s; my teaching of English to international students in Australia; and my observations of an exceptional intervention of a young Gondi-speaking teacher in the poor outskirts of Bhopal, in India. Each of the three contexts is characterised by multilingualism within the community. Each is also characterised by a tension between what the education authorities and mainstream curriculum suggest is the appropriate way of teaching languages and the whole curriculum, and a reflexive alternative based on the rediscovery of translation.

Reclaiming the Value of Translation

The three examples show that the multilingualism and multilinguality of students, teachers and teacher educators are resources which can lead to innovative teaching and learning opportunities. These opportunities arise from a context in which teachers and students consciously test the boundaries of what are viewed by educational authorities as conventional language practices. The context is also one in which the three sets of agents reflect on conventional practices, find them inadequate, and take reflexive action to establish new ways of enhancing learning by tapping into the repository of language knowledge which students have.

Language practices in in-service teacher education programme for multilingual education

Following political change in South Africa in 1994, a democratic constitution set out the principles of an eleven official language policy and the further development of multilingualism in the country. This was followed by a new education policy: language education policy (DoE 1997a) and curriculum and assessment policy (DoE 1997b). Immediately thereafter, the Project for the Study of Alternative Education in South Africa (PRAESA) based at the University of Cape Town, in the Western Cape Province, initiated an in-service, Further Diploma in Multilingual Education (FDE) for practising teachers. The intention was to support the multilingual education policy by preparing teachers to implement the new multilingual policy in their classrooms.

There are three main languages in the Western Cape Province: Afrikaans, Xhosa and English. There are also many minority languages, including other South African languages as well as the languages of various migrant communities, many of which have come from other African countries since the mid-1990s. Multilingualism in South Africa, as in India, is not simply a matter of multiple languages; it is also a matter of the ways in which people use their language skills (multilinguality) to navigate between and among different languages and communities (Agnihotri 2007).

The in-service teacher education programme was to offer a one-year enrichment diploma for practising teachers. The teachers encountered students from two or more language backgrounds in their classrooms and these students were also required to learn two or three languages at school. For most students this meant a transition from home language (mother tongue) to English medium education by the fourth grade. However, it was anticipated that the new language policy would be implemented in such a way that within a few years, all students would receive a minimum of six years of education in the home language (mother tongue) before the transition to English.[1]

Most of the teachers in the programme were speakers of Xhosa or Afrikaans, with varying degrees of proficiency in English. Most programmes of this university are offered in English medium and the teachers who enrolled were enthusiastic and excited about studying through English. Apart from participating in a teacher upgrading programme which would give them greater job security and an increase in salary, they were enthusiastic about the opportunity to enhance their own proficiency in English.

Since the intention of the programme was to introduce teachers to multilingual theory and pedagogy, each teacher was required to take a course in the further development of one of the languages which they needed to use in the schooling system. Most of the lectures were delivered in English, but students were always encouraged to use Xhosa and Afrikaans in class discussions and to use the language of their preference when asking questions. Xhosa and Afrikaans were frequently used for clarifications and in small group work activities. To be honest, we were 'preaching multilingual education' mainly through English, and not enough use was made of Afrikaans and English in the lecturing process. This was because while all the lecturing staff were fluent in English there were varying degrees of proficiency in Xhosa and Afrikaans and most of the readings were available only in English.

Fairly soon it became apparent that many of the teachers experienced difficulty in writing university assignments. Most academic material on teacher education and also that which deals with bilingual and multilingual education has been written in English or other international languages. In our context, students therefore had to work with academic material in English. Unsurprisingly, student assignments included long extracts of material inadequately attributed or referenced and it was not clear to the teaching staff

[1] In fact this has not occurred because the government authorities have not yet implemented the language policy and the curriculum proceeds as if an early-transition to English were not problematic. As it happens, this practice is highly problematic and student achievement suffers as a result (Heugh 2009).

how much of this material was really understood by the students (in-service teachers). The university response would normally have been to accuse the students of plagiarism and to fail assignments such as these. We thought about this a great deal and we realised that the teachers had no other recourse but to use the vocabulary and academic syntax of the original authors because they did not have the necessary academic vocabulary and syntax in English to write in English.

So the teacher development team went back to old educational practices of Socrates, Plato and Aristotle. We used the Socratic Method to discuss the problem, from every angle with the students, and finally came up with a solution. This was to ask the students who had resorted to 'plagiarism' to rewrite the assignments in their home language, whether this was Xhosa or Afrikaans. In effect we were relying on Plato's assumption that everyone has knowledge or is born with knowledge and Aristotle's belief that experience and expertise are what is important. We knew that the teachers had funds of knowledge which they could tap and several years of teaching experience, and that these could be brought to bear in their discussion of literature on multilingual education, language acquisition and pedagogy.

At first the teachers were reluctant to try this. Some claimed that they could not write in an academic way in Xhosa, for example, because they thought that African languages were not sufficiently well-developed for this to occur. Together we came up with a way around this, and that was for the students to use the 'academic terminology in English' but to discuss what it meant and to write their essays in either Xhosa or Afrikaans. Once the students had done this, they reported that for the first time they felt confident that they could contribute something useful in a written assignment.

Since this had seemed to be a worthwhile process, we asked all students, not only those who had struggled with the first assignment, to follow this approach for the second assignment. Writing in either Afrikaans or Xhosa meant that plagiarism from the English texts was virtually impossible. The teachers had to make use of their own translation skills and to develop these further. More than this, they had to develop their skills in paraphrasing, summarising, and also in providing critical commentary in the language of their greatest use.

Using their more familiar language in their writing permitted the students to bring their own knowledge and experience to the written discussion. What we found was that the written assignments were far more richly nuanced and more substantive when the teachers wrote in their home language or language of greatest fluency. As a third step, we considered asking the students to translate their essays written mostly in Xhosa or Afrikaans into English, without going back to the academic literary texts, and thus to avoid the temptation to rely again on the constructions of the original authors. Although this did happen in a few cases, this part of the process was not carried through systematically.[2]

What we as teacher educators learnt was that we were better able to assess the teachers' engagement with the literature. Their translations, interpretation, paraphrasing, summarising and critiquing of the source texts from English into their home language provided clear evidence of their skills at processing the literature and relating this to their own teaching experiences. Of course, this initiative presented a challenge in regard to grading assessments. Collectively the teacher education team members each had at least two languages: English-Afrikaans, with a little Xhosa, or Xhosa-English with a little Afrikaans. The team members had to rethink their own responses and assessment practices. This resulted in staff using their own bilingualism or multilingualism and also working in pairs where necessary to discuss and grade each assessment. Since we were working in pairs and using our different language skills, the process involved negotiation of meaning between each pair of staff and this in turn resulted in a heightened awareness of our own 'multilinguality' as well as our own shortcomings. An unanticipated benefit to students was that feedback on assignments was provided on an individual basis and from the pair of tutors who graded the each assignment. Students were given an opportunity to clarify parts of the assignment and this sometimes resulted in moderated grades.

[2] The FDE in multilingual education was offered from 1997–2000 (over four years), but because the government failed to take any steps towards implementing the multilingual schools policy, the University of Cape Town discontinued this programme.

This process was beneficial both to the teachers and teacher educators as it encouraged a reflexive process and one which we hoped the teachers would be able to model with their own students in the school classroom. What this process taught the teachers was that if they had difficulty writing academic essays in English, then the situation for their own school students was even more problematic. The process of writing assignments in Xhosa, particularly, empowered the teachers to understand that school students could engage in academic thought and writing in their home language and that this process did not have to be conducted through English. In effect, the teacher education process involved negotiation of practice between the trainers and the teachers and it involved reflexivity on the part of all the stakeholders.

The university, predominantly and historically English-medium, was initially skeptical and reluctant to accept this approach. The university authorities claimed that they would not be able to conduct their quality control procedures or verify assignment records and grades if assignments were not written in English. However, this was at a historical period in which the multilingual imperatives within the constitution were very much in the public domain. Secondly, since each of the teacher educators was technically employed by the university and therefore assumed to be equipped to teach and assess students, the university was unable to produce sufficiently convincing grounds to prevent the practice from continuing while this programme was offered at the institution.

Using translation with international students to enhance academic developing in English

Ten years later I found myself teaching English to international students at the University of South Australia. While most of the students in these courses come from China, Korea, Hong Kong and Malaysia, there are also students from Japan, India, Sudan, Ethiopia, Liberia, Egypt, Saudi Arabia, Iraq, Chile, and several European countries. So the classes are characterised by the linguistic diversity of the students. I inherited courses which used a mix of ESL and EFL methodologies, with a significant emphasis on grammar (based on

Michael Halliday's 'Systemic Functional Linguistics'). The approach to writing was based on a formulaic interpretation of the 'genre' approach to writing which has become popular in Australia. Students found these courses boring and repetitive, and so did I.

Most of the students who participate in these courses have difficulty with writing university essays and assignments. A common difficulty is that the readings that students are required to use in their essays are written with a high density of passive constructions, very long noun strings (nominalisations), especially at the beginning of sentences, and finally, unnecessarily complex vocabulary. Just as the teachers in South Africa resorted to lifting chunks of the original author's text and inserting these into their essays, so did many (or most) of the students I have been teaching in Australia. So I tried various different strategies to avoid placing students into a situation which leaves them with little alternative but to 'plagiarise'.

The first strategy was to insist on hand-written assignments in class, without access to electronic instruments. This certainly removed the option to 'copy and paste', and it has encouraged students to get used to the idea of writing, regularly in class. A second strategy was to insist that the students write regular entries on a discussion site on the course website. Here students can respond to weekly tasks, usually requiring interpretation and reflection on weekly readings. I respond to each of these entries but never correct grammar or spelling, so students can write without being fearful of seeing corrections, and they can view each other's contributions and 'mistakes'. This has had the effect of reducing anxiety about writing. However, I still found that the students did not seem to be making the kind of progress in their English writing that I know is necessary for them to succeed in other courses at this university.

So I began to draw students' attention to their own cognitive processes when making meaning and transferring meaning between their languages, particularly in regards to translation in writing. For example, in one first year assignment, students are expected to interview someone in the community and then to write up a biography of this person's life. Along with the final draft of this assignment, students are required to collate all of their research material, including transcripts of interviews, interview notes and draft assignments, and to submit every bit of evidence of their project work in a folder. I encourage students to take interview notes in whichever language or languages seem to be appropriate. I also encourage students to use whichever languages are appropriate in their planning of the written task and in their drafts. For example, they are encouraged to write in English but that when they get stuck, to include words or phrases in their home language, in order to keep going. I ask that they show me how they revise their texts by converting the parts in their home language into English. Students have adopted various strategies which range from writing up everything in their home language first and then translating into English, to writing everything in English, and various strategies in between.

At first the students told me that they had been forbidden to do this in all of their earlier English language courses, so they were reluctant to try this out. They had been told to think in English only and not to think in their home language. Nevertheless, about half of the students did use various translation strategies, and their biographies were more substantial and more nuanced than those of the other students. Those who elected to write only in English wrote shorter, more predictable and pedestrian texts, with more 'grammatical errors' than were evident in the work of students who used translation. Those who have used more translation inform me that they found the process rewarding and the quality of their written work in English is markedly different at the end of the course than it was at the beginning of the semester.

Translation of learning and teaching materials from English to Hindi and Gondi

In September 2012, a number of teachers and community educators attended a week-long workshop on language hosted by Eklavya, in Bhopal. During this workshop, bilingual and multilingual educations were the focus of attention. At the end of the workshop I had the privilege of visiting a few schools and education centres in poor areas on the outskirts of the city. At one of these, a young Gondi-speaking teacher, who had been at the workshop, worked with marginalised Gondi-speaking children who were not in formal education. The centre had a range of teaching and learning resources, mainly in Hindi and English. During the visit to the centre, the young teacher very shyly took some materials that she had developed herself out of a drawer in her desk. They comprised materials that she had translated from the internet into both Gondi and Hindi. She had hand-written the materials, used pictures downloaded from the internet, laminated them, and collated them in a plastic ring binder. What was extraordinary about this was that the teacher had not known about the value of bilingual or multilingual education when she had developed these materials some time earlier; she had simply done this herself because she thought it made sense. It made sense because she could see that the children in her care were not responding to learning to read and write in Hindi and she realised that they would have a better opportunity to develop reading and writing in Gondi and Hindi simultaneously—thereby building on their knowledge of two language systems used in their neighbourhood.

Conclusion

This chapter illustrates three different settings in which teachers or teacher educators have been faced with multilingual learners and language education systems which do not meet the needs of the learners well enough. In each case, the teachers turned to translation. Behind translation lies the actual mechanics and processes of language learning which have been largely ignored for several decades. Recent discussions which focus on language as a process rather than an object, for example in the work of Merill Swain who uses the term 'languaging' (Swain 2006); and further discussions of how languaging occurs between different language systems, 'translanguaging' (García 2009) are closely connected to Agnihotri's (2006, 2007, 2009, 2014) understanding of 'multilinguality'. It seems to me that two obvious dimensions of translanguaging are translation and interpreting, and that there is every reason to make more use of translation to strengthen language development. What is particularly useful is that translation simultaneously strengthens language development in each of the languages being used in the process.

References

Agnihotri, Rama Kant, (2006). 'Identity and multilinguality: The case of India'. In A. B. M. Tsui & J. W. Tollefson (eds), *Language policy, Culture, and Identity in Asian Contexts*. Mahwah, NJ: Lawrence Erlbaum Associates, Inc., 185–204.

——— (2007). 'Towards a pedagogical paradigm rooted in multilinguality'. *International Multilingual Research Journal*, 1/2, 79–88.

——— (2009). 'Multilinguality and a new world order'. In A. K. Mohanty, M. Panda, R. Phillipson, and T. Skutnabb-Kangas (eds), *Multilingual Education for Social Justice: Globalizing the Local*. New Delhi: Orient BlackSwan, 268–77.

——— (2014). 'Multilinguality, education and harmony'. *International Journal of Multilingualism*, doi: 10.1080/14790718.2014.921181

Department of Education, (1997a). *Language in Education Policy*. Pretoria: Department of Education.

Department of Education, (1997b). *Curriculum 2005. Lifelong Learning for the 21st Century*. Pretoria: Department of Education.

García, Ofelia, (2009). *Bilingual Education in the 21st Century: A Global Perspective*. Oxford: Wiley-Blackwell.

Heugh, Kathleen, (2009). 'Literacy and bi/multilingual education in Africa: Recovering collective memory and knowledge'. In Ajit Mohanty, Minati Panda, Robert Phillipson and Tove Skutnabb-Kangas (eds), *Multilingual Education for Social Justice: Globalising the Local*. New Delhi: Orient BlackSwan, 95–113.

Hymes, D. H., (1972). 'On communicative competence'. In J. B. Pride & J. Holmes (eds), *Sociolinguistics*. London: Penguin, 269–93.

Stroud, Christopher & Kathleen Heugh, (2011). 'Language education'. In R. Mesthrie (ed.), *Cambridge Handbook of Sociolinguistics*. Cambridge: Cambridge University Press. 413–29.

Swain, Merill, (2006). 'Language, agency and collaboration in advanced second language proficiency'. In Heidi Byrnes (ed.), *Advanced Language Learning: The Contribution of Halliday and Vygotsky*. London: Continuum, 95–108.

CHAPTER 3

Innovations in Research and Teaching in Multilingual Classrooms

MUKUL SAXENA

ABSTRACT

This paper aims to foreground the theoretical developments in research on innovative teaching practices in multilingual classrooms that have taken place during the last three decades. It reviews three generations of studies that document innovations, or lack of them, in multilingual classroom practices: the first generation of research in multilingual and multicultural classroom contexts that grew out of the field of linguistic anthropology in North America; the second generation of studies, emerging from the early 1990s onwards, that developed critical, interpretive approaches to the study of multilingual classroom interaction; and the third generation of studies that are opening up new epistemological spaces at the interface with other fields of research, such as multimodality in classroom interaction or ethnography of language policy, while building on the robust foundation of the first and second generations of research. The review documents product oriented research focusing on language-in-education policy to process oriented research exploring learner-centered, collaborating classrooms to unpack the agentive roles of teachers and learners and the dialogic nature of structure and agency.

INTRODUCTION

The ethnography of policy is a distinctive and growing tradition of research on multilingual classroom discourse. It is built on the solid foundation of three decades of research which Saxena & Martin-Jones (2013) have called three generations of research. This paper charts the journey from product oriented and policy driven quantitative research to qualitative research focusing on discourse analyses and ethnography of policy. The latter interpretivist tradition documents both teacher-dominated classroom interaction and learner-centred and collaborative classroom interactions that value linguistic and cultural diversity in the classroom. This paper aims to review and foreground developments in research that captures innovative teaching practices in multilingual classrooms.

First Generation Research

Until the early 1980s, large-scale positivist-oriented research on language-in-education policies and bilingual education programme outcomes focused on students' developing proficiency in different languages and on their 'levels' of achievement across the curriculum. In contrast to this quantitative *product* oriented research, in the late 1980s, the first generation of research focused on the *processes* of multilingual classroom interaction. They were qualitative research approaches and therefore, represented a major paradigm shift. This research among anthropological linguists in North America grew out of a widely held concern, in the 1970s and early 1980s, about the education of children from linguistic and cultural minority groups. The research reflected the broad epistemological turn towards a focus on language as a form of social action and towards research of a qualitative and interpretive nature. It was grounded in a number of interrelated approaches to language in social life: micro-ethnography (Erickson 1975), ethnomethodology (Mehan 1979, 1981), ethnography of communication (Hymes 1964), interactional sociolinguistics (Gumperz 1982) and the sociology of face-to-face interaction (Goffman 1981).

A generation of studies, emerging from the early 1990s onwards, developed critical, interpretive approaches to the study of multilingual classroom interaction. These approaches incorporated two main perspectives: critical approaches to ethnography (e.g.,

Canagarajah 1993, 1999; McCarty 2002; Stroud 2003; Lin & Martin 2005; Ramanathan 2005), and post-structuralist and post-modern perspectives (e.g., Heller 1994, 1999; Martin-Jones & Saxena 1995; Martin-Jones & Heller 1996; Arthur 1996; Lin 1996, 1999; Jaffe 1999; Heller & Martin-Jones 2001). These studies were carried out in much wider research sites geographically: classroom-based research in post-colonial contexts, minority language contexts in Europe and Indigenous and minority language contexts in the USA and Canada. In contrast to the first generation studies, these new studies were explicitly framed in relation to language-in-education policy.

Second Generation Research

Through micro-level analysis of multilingual classroom discourse, the second generation research showed tensions between the top down language-in-education policies and the achievement of effective teaching and learning (e.g., Canagarajah 2001; McGlynn & Martin 2009; Arthur Shoba 2010). Their findings suggest that in many contexts, particularly the post-colonial, the monolingual ideologies of one-language-only are the guiding principle for the prescriptive language education policies (Phillipson 1992; Lin & Martin 2005; Li Wei & Martin 2009; Saxena 2009). Consequently, many teachers associate the use of L1 in the classroom with underachievement and enforce 'L2/English-only' policies. This is despite the fact that there is no evidence to support it (Eldridge 1996; Grima 2001; Baetens Beardsmore 2003).

The research in post-colonial multilingual countries (e.g., Lin 1996; Arthur 2001; Canagarajah 2001; Hornberger & Chick 2001; Lin & Martin, 2005) demonstrated that the local dominant ideologies are often pitted against the 'English-only' ideology which is considered to have its origins in 'the English Language Teaching (ELT) institutions of the centre that influence language education policy making around the world' (Canagarajah 2001:194). It is also found that the socio-cultural sanctity of the English classrooms and linguistic purism are often challenged by bilingual teachers and students in order to accomplish the task of effective teaching-learning. Therefore, rather than passively submitting to the 'English-only' ideology, they actively negotiate in their code-switching practices the opposing ideologies associated with the teaching of English-only and the local/ national languages. For example, I have shown in my research on higher secondary classrooms in Brunei Darussalam how the essentialisation of the English classrooms' socio-cultural spaces as non-local is met with resistance. This resistance, as can be seen in an interaction below, is manifested in the form of sociolinguistic practices of L1 use for pedagogic and symbolic functions (see for details, Saxena, 2009).

[T=teacher, S1=identified student, SS=students, <E>=the utterance in *normal* font following this sign is uttered in English, <M>=the utterance in *bold* is in Malay, { }= contains translation of Malay utterances, non-verbal communication, or researcher's comment]

T: what's a VILLAGE^
SS: {some mumbling}
T: what is a village^
S1: ( )<M>**kampung** ( ) {*village*} {laughs}
SS: {laughter}
T: <E> umm in English please this is not a Malay lesson
S2: people live
T: RIGHT where many people live okay…and in olden days …

In this extract, after uttering the Malay word '**kampung**' (meaning village) in L1 in line 56, the student (S1) 'laughs' and along with him (in line 57) the rest of the students (SS) laugh too. As a consequence of the classroom management talk established by the teacher (T) since the previous year, the students were aware of and were constantly reminded about the 'no Malay rule' by the teacher (as in Line 58). Following the teacher's departure from the class, when I had an informal chat with the students, they told me that they knew the Malay equivalent of the word 'village' (as shown in line 56, with 'some mumbling') but did not know how to define the word in English. They knew they were not supposed to reply in

Malay, but the one who did, did it anyway, as he said, 'to annoy the teacher'. These students and others, as revealed by my ethnographic research in English classrooms (Saxena 2007, 2008, 2009, 2010), found the marginalisation of their national language, Malay, in English classrooms very confusing. This confusion derived from the fact that Malay as the national language was venerated in different forms and practices symbolic of their Brunei Malay cultural and traditional identity. The cultural socialisation of children at home, in the community, mosques and schools driven by the national ideology (Saxena 2008), also led them to challenge the 'policing English' policy which they saw as marginalising their home/community and national language.

The symbolic function of L1 use, what I called as 'non-cooperative' resistance (Saxena 2009), also serves to highlight the fact that teachers, whose views are shaped by the 'English-only' ideology, problematise English and, therefore, unwittingly position it as 'the linguistic other'. This ideological conflict of national and global ideologies reflects the post-colonial dilemma of internationalisation and localisation. In contrast, there are many other English classrooms in Brunei that negotiate this ideological conflict in their code-switching practices in the classroom. In doing so, they can be seen as resisting the 'othering' of Malay.

T: tomarctus. Roam <M>**apalagi nya**{*what else*}<E> what did it say with roam^
SS: <E> Roam
T: What's…the meaning of "roam"…
S?: ( )
T: <M> Nooo
S?: <M>**Apakan**^ {*What* ^}
S?: <M>…**Apakan**^ {*What* ^}
T: <E>Roam, what does "roam" means
S?: <E>…Roam <M>**kah mcm** … {*like what…*}
S?: Rarrrr…
T: <E> No that's "Roa..red"
S?: <E> "Roam around" <M>**bah**…{*It's "roam around"*}
T1: <E>Roaming **bah**… *It's roaming…*

S?: <M>**Ah...chatu bah**...{*Aaa like that...*}
T: <M>...**mcm kalau telipun**.....{*it's like if a phone*}<E> it would, you know, roaming, right^
S?: <E> "Roaming" <M>**kah ^**{*Do you mean "roaming"^*}
S?: ˙Mm
S?: <M>**Ah...bulih**...{*Aaa...is that so...*}
S?: <E>**Buleh kan tu** ^ {*Can it so* ^}
T: <M> ...**kalau binatang** ... {*if animals*}<E> they roam around^ <M> **Macam bejalan-jalan**. {*Like going around*} <E>You know^
S?: <M>**Cari makan bah 'cher**... {*They're simply looking for food...*}

In contrast to the interaction in the previous classroom (Classroom 1), here (Classroom 2) we can see that the teacher (T) and the students jointly unravel the meaning of a text bilingually. Here, as a consequence of 'bilingual supportive scaffolding' (Saxena 2010) facilitated by the teacher, the participants are negotiating the meaning of the word 'roam' with the help of code-switching. After a few failed attempts at identifying the meaning, a student in line 37 exclaims 'Roam around' <M>**bah**...{*It's 'roam around'*}, 'bah' being a Malay particle used in Brunei English (Cornard 1990). As the ensuing interaction shows, this utterance orients the teacher and the other learners to roaming with respect to mobile phones to which Bruneians, as an affluent society, were quite accustomed. The use of Malay allows fluidity in the conversation and achieves 'reciprocity of perspective or meaning' (Edwards and Furlong 1987) between the teacher and the learners. This is a telling example of how teachers are able to exploit the linguistic and cultural capital (Bourdieu 1977, 1991) as 'funds of knowledge' (Moll et al. 1992; Martin-Jones & Saxena, 2003) when L1 is not positioned as the 'linguistic other' in the classroom. Within the top-down language-in-education policies of the education ministry, here we see the teacher and learners 'opening and filling up implementation spaces' in the top-down policies (Hornberger 2005) which are 'socially constructed and dynamically negotiated on a moment-by-moment basis' (García & Menken 2010: 257). The 'bilingual scaffolding' (Saxena 2010) that the teacher provides allows 'translanguaging' (García 2009; Creese & Blackledge 2010), practices of switching between languages in the classroom and thus challenging top-down institutional arrangements. By 'slicing through' the layers of a language policy 'onion', what this type of second generation research (Martin-Jones & Saxena 1995; Lin 1996; Arthur 2001; Canagarajah 2001; Hornberger & Chick 2001) has shown is 'to reveal agentive spaces in which local actors implement, interpret and perhaps resist policy initiatives' (Hornberger & Johnson 2007: 509), rather than simply focusing on the policies that are handed down from above. This is what I have called participants engaging in 'constructive resistance' (Saxena 2009) which is productive, in contrast to the 'non-cooperative resistance' like we see in Classroom 1.

Third Generation Research

In the third generation of research, we see some continuity with the first and second generation studies. A special issue of *Language and Education* (Saxena & Martin-Jones, 2013) brought together researchers who are now part of a third generation of scholars currently involved in studies of multilingual classroom interaction. All of these research studies have taken on board the concerns of researchers working in the newly established field of ethnography of language policy (Ricento & Hornberger 1996; Hornberger & Johnson 2007; Johnson 2009; McCarty 2011), drawing on rich insights from ethnographic work into the rigour of close discourse-analytic research. The continuity can be seen: in the foregrounding of situated practices and meaning-making in interaction; in the emphasis on the agency exercised by teachers and students, as key social actors in policy-making processes; and in the concern with the ways in which interactional practices and classroom routines index wider language ideologies. In addition to continuity with earlier generations of research, we also see the opening up of new epistemological spaces at the interface with other fields of research (e.g., multimodality in classroom interaction). For example, Budach's (2013) article opens up for us a key innovative dimension of classroom interaction in primary school settings in Germany: namely multilingual talk around artifacts or objects and their use as semiotic resources in their own right.

Budach's article draws on her research in a German-Italian two-way-immersion classroom in Frankfurt, Germany. The focus of the analysis is on objects and their role in shaping language practices and social interaction. Budach shows, with a fine-grained attention to analytic detail, the norm of language separation governing the speech economy of each classroom was not always upheld in the ebb and flow of spontaneous classroom talk. In fact, when occasional shifts occurred towards the use of 'bilingual resources' for meaning-making and knowledge-building, this led to a weaker teacher framing of the classroom interaction and allowed more space for the children to exercise agency. Moreover, particular kinds of classroom activities, such as those organised around objects or artifacts brought to class by the children, provided rich opportunities for bilingual classroom conversations of a learner-centred nature. Budach proposes the adoption of an analytic framework that takes account of the interplay of multilingual and multimodal resources in different kinds of teaching/learning events. She also reminds us of the need to take account of the specific nature of the pedagogy observable in different multilingual classrooms settings.

The articles in the aforementioned special volume of *Language and Education* provide very good exemplars of third generation studies in different multilingual classroom settings. First, they took research on multilingual classroom interaction into new educational domains and, in doing so, draw our attention to new dimensions of multilingual classroom talk and multilingual/ multimodal pedagogy. Take, for example, in her case study of an induction class for newly-arrived immigrant children in France, Bonacina-Pugh (2013) shows how language choices indexed 'teacher-hood', or 'doing being' the teacher, and she provides a vivid illustration of the ways in which the classroom participants (teacher and students) played creatively with the performance of 'teacher-hood', allowing multiple language resources to be brought into the interaction. Here, we see the agency exercised by the teacher and the students in opening up a space for multilingual ways of teaching and learning. Bonacina-Pugh calls this a 'practiced language policy'.

In another setting, Libya, Asker & Martin-Jones (2013) show through a close analysis of the use of Berber in 'on-stage' and 'off-stage' conversations how the teachers in two classes differed in the ways in which they navigated the school's Arabic-only policy, with one teacher strictly upholding the policy and the other teacher adopting a more relaxed approach to the use of Berber by the students. They also show the ways in which the students varied in their use of Arabic, Berber and English. Profiling two students in particular, they illustrate the ways in which they navigated the norms of multilingual classroom interaction and the constraints of the school language policy. One student alternated skilfully between the uses of Arabic and English in interacting with her teacher and used Berber only with her peers. Another used Berber as a resource for engaging in 'small acts of resistance' to the teacher's agenda. In this study, we see multilingual classroom practices similar to what I presented earlier in the context of Brunei Darussalam in South-East Asia.

Boon's study (2013) moves us away from the primary and secondary school contexts and enters two adult literacy classes in the small, multilingual nation of Timor-Leste, in South-East Asia. Here, we see an even wider range of multilingual resources being drawn upon in classroom talk, for example, the articulation of letter names in different languages, viz., Portuguese, Tetun and Bahasa Indonesia. Boon reveals the differences between the linguistic and pedagogic practices of the two literacy teachers. While both of them orient to the use of Tetun as the main 'on-stage' language of the class, they draw on different multilingual resources in giving feedback to class participants or in engaging in small talk with individuals, because their own communicative repertoires have been shaped in different ways by their educational trajectories and patterns of residence.

As with other third generation studies, the research reported in the special issue is also opening up promising new epistemological spaces at the interface with recent research in cognate fields. This includes the interface with research in new literacy studies (Boon 2013), multimodal classroom communication (Budach 2013), conversational analysis of code-switching (Bonacina-Pugh 2013), and language ideology (Chimbutane 2013; Asker & Martin-Jones 2013). All the studies here complement the research being developed in the new field of ethnography of language policy. They also use similar research lenses. The analyses of multilingual classroom interaction are grounded in extended ethnographic engagement with participants and in insights gleaned from ethnographic interviews, taking full account of emic perspectives. In these different classroom settings, we see ample evidence of teacher and student agency, in relaxing policy prescriptions, in engaging in small acts of resistance, in creative play and in the use of multimodal resources. We also see the traces of past and present language-in-education policies. And, tellingly, an ideological orientation to monolingual ways of working in schools and classrooms surfaces across the different research sites, even in the bilingual education programmes. In each case, we get glimpses of the wider worlds beyond the classroom and disadvantage suffered by learners in education systems which, shaped by colonial pasts and by globalisation forces in the present day, perpetuate this 'dual focus'.

Constructive Resistance in the Classroom

In many classrooms, where there is a lack of adequate professional preparation, teachers have no option but to reproduce restrictive pedagogies to which they themselves were exposed to as learners. We observe the lack of agentive response from teachers to the needs of the learners in Classroom 1 in Brunei Darussalam, in one of the classrooms in Libya by Asker & Martin-Jones (2013), and in the use of Portuguese and Changana at the primary level in Mozambique by Chimbutane (2013). While second and third generation research reveal overwhelming presence of this deterministic view of passive teachers, it also shows glimpses of practices of 'constructive resistance' (Saxena 2009) to top-down policies by the teachers, negotiating conflicting ideologies of localisation and globalisation in their code-switching practices in multilingual classrooms. The learner-centred approach to teaching, as observed, for example, in Classroom 2 in

Brunei Darussalam and by Budach (2013) in Germany and by other second and third generation of researchers in diverse geographical contexts, requires innovative interactional practices which provide agentive powers to teachers and opportunities to the learners for engagement with their teachers in the construction of knowledge in specific contexts and affirming their identities. Teacher training for classes with multilingual participants need to inculcate that the use of more than one language demands strategic code-switching grounded in the 'neo-Vygotskyan approach' (Mercer 1994, 2004) to understanding the role of language and talk in co-construction of knowledge and cognitive and linguistic development. The theoretical notion of 'bilingual supportive scaffolding' (Saxena 2010) that combines neo-Vygotskyan approach with the critical perspective and the ethnography of policy approach, and draws on the notions of 'translanguaging' (García 2009), 'funds of knowledge' (Moll et al. 1992) and 'constructive resistance' (Saxena 2009), plays a central role in constructing understanding for teachers and researchers about the innovative practices associated with learner-centred approaches. Teacher education programmes need to take on board these theoretical developments and the innovative practices in multilingual classrooms that they are capable of capturing.

References

Arthur, J., (1996). 'Code-switching and collusion: Classroom interaction in Botswana primary schools'. *Linguistics and Education*, 8/1, 17–34.

——— (2001). 'Code-switching and collusion: Classroom interaction in Botswana primary schools'. M. Heller & M. Martin-Jones (eds), 57–76.

——— (2010). 'Scottish classroom voices: A case study of teaching and learning Scots. *Language and Education*, 24/5, 385–400.

Asker, A. & M. Martin-Jones, (2013). '"A classroom is not a classroom if students are talking to me in Berber": Language ideologies and multilingual resources in secondary school English classes in Libya'. *Language and Education*, 27/4, 343–55.

Baetens Beardsmore, H., (2003). 'Who's afraid of bilingualism?' In J. Dewaele, A. Housen & Li Wei (eds), *Bilingualism: Beyond Basic Principles*. Clevedon, UK: Multilingual Matters, 10–27.

Bonacina-Pugh, R., (2013). 'Categories and language choice in the multilingual classroom: The relevance of "teacher-hood"'. *Language and Education*, 27/4, 298–313.

Boon, D., (2013). 'Multilingual classroom talk in adult literacy education in Timor-Leste: Teachers and learners doing literacy and numeracy tasks'. *Language and Education*, 27/4, 356–73.

Bourdieu, P., 1977. 'The economics of linguistics exchange'. *Social Science Information*, 16/6, 45–68.

——— (1991). *Language and Symbolic Power.* Cambridge, MA: Harvard University Press.

Budach, G., (2013). 'From language choice to mode choice: How artefacts impact on language use and the creation of meaning in a bilingual classroom'. *Language and Education*, 27/4, 329–42.

Canagarajah, A.S., 1993. 'Critical ethnography of a Sri Lankan classroom: Ambiguities in student opposition to reproduction through ESOL'. *TESOL Quarterly*, 27, 601–26.

——— (1999). *Resisting Linguistic Imperialism in English Teaching*. Oxford: Oxford University Press.

——— (2001). 'Constructing hybrid post-colonial subjects: Code-switching in Jaffna classrooms'. In M. Heller & M. Martin-Jones (eds), 193–212.

Chimbutane, F., (2013). 'Code-switching in L1 and L2 learning contexts: Beliefs and practices in Mozambican bilingual education schools'. *Language and Education*, 27/4, 314–28.

Creese, A. & A. Blackledge, (2010). 'Translanguaging in the bilingual classroom: A pedagogy for learning and teaching?' *Modern Languages Journal*, 94/1, 103–15.

Conrad, A., (1990). 'The BAH Particle in Brunei English'. *RELC Journal*, 21, 14–28.

Edwards, A. & V. J. Furlong, (1987). 'Teaching and learning as the creation of meanings'. In B. Mayor & A. Pugh (eds), *Language, Communication and Education*. London: Croom Helm, 357–70.

Eldridge, J., (1996). 'Code-switching in a Turkish secondary school'. *ELT Journal*, 50/54, 303–11.

Erickson, F., (1975). 'Gatekeeping and the melting pot: Interaction in counselling encounters'. *Harvard Educational Review*, 45, 44–70.

García, O., (2009). *Bilingual Education in the 21st Century*. Oxford: Wiley-Blackwell.

García, O. & K. Menken, (2010). 'Stirring the onion: Educators and the dynamics of language education policies (looking ahead)'. In K.

Menken & O. García (eds), *Negotiating Language Policies in Schools: Educators as Policymakers*. New York: Routledge, 249–61.

Goffman, E., (1981). *Forms of Talk*. Philadelphia: University of Pennsylvania Press.

Grima, A., (2001). 'Language values and identities: Code-switching in secondary classrooms in Malta'. In M. Heller & M. Martin-Jones (eds), 213–34.

Gumperz, J. J., (1982). *Discourse Strategies*. Cambridge: Cambridge University Press.

Heller, M., (1994). *Crosswords: Language, Education and Ethnicity in French Ontario*. Berlin: Mouton de Gruyter.

——— (1999). *Linguistic Minorities and Modernity*. London: Longman. (Second edition, 2006, Continuum).

Heller, M. & M. Martin-Jones (eds), (2001). *Voices of Authority: Education and Linguistic Difference.* Westport, CT: Ablex.

Hornberger, N. H., (2005). 'Opening and filling up implementational and ideological spaces in heritage language education'. *Modern Languages Journal*, 89/4, 605–09.

Hornberger, N. H. & J. K. Chick, (2001). 'Co-constructing school safetime: Safetalk practices in Peruvian and South African classrooms'. In M. Heller & M. Martin-Jones, 31–55.

Hornberger, N. H. & D. C. Johnson, (2007). 'Slicing the onion ethnographically: Layers and spaces in multilingual language policy and practice'. *TESOL Quarterly*, 41, 509–32.

Hymes, D., (1964). 'Introduction: Towards ethnographies of communication'. *American Anthropologist*, 66/6/II, 1–34.

Jaffe, A., (1999). *Ideologies in Action: Language Politics on Corsica*. Berlin: Mouton de Gruyter.

Johnson, D. C., (2009). 'Ethnography of language policy'. *Language Policy*, 8/2, 139–59.

Li Wei, & P. Martin, (2009). 'Conflicts and tensions in classroom code-switching: An introduction'. *International Journal of Bilingual Education and Bilingualism*, 12/2, 117–22.

Lin, A. M. Y., (1996). 'Bilingualism or linguistic segregation? Symbolic domination, resistance and code-switching'. *Linguistics and Education*, 8/1, 49–84.

——— (1999). 'Doing-English-lessons in the reproduction or transformation of social worlds'. *TESOL Quarterly*, 33, 393–412.

Lin, A. M. Y. & P. W. Martin (eds), (2005). *Decolonisation, Globalisation:*

Language-in-Education Policy and Practice. Clevedon, Avon: Multilingual Matters.

Martin-Jones, M. & M. Saxena, (1995). 'Supporting or containing bilingualism? Policies, power asymmetries and pedagogic practices in mainstream primary classrooms'. In J. W. Tollefson (ed.), *Language, Power and Inequality*. New York: Cambridge University Press, 73–90.

——— (2003). 'Bilingual resources and "funds of knowledge" for teaching and learning in multi-ethnic classes in Britain'. *International Journal of Bilingual Education and Bilingualism*, 6/3–4, 267–82.

Martin-Jones, M. & M. Heller, (1996). 'Introduction to the special issue on education in multilingual settings: Discourse, identities and power. Part 1: Constructing legitimacy'. *Linguistics and Education*, 8/1, 1–16.

McCarty, T. L., (2002). *A place to be Navajo: Rough Rock and the Struggle for Self-Determination in Indigenous Schooling*. Mahwah, NJ: Lawrence Erlbaum.

——— (ed.), (2011). *Ethnography of Language Policy*. New York: Routledge.

McGlynn, C. & P. W. Martin, (2009). '"No vernacular": Tensions in language choice in a sexual health lesson in The Gambia'. *International Journal of Bilingualism and Bilingual Education*, 12/2, 137–55.

Mehan, H., (1979). *Learning Lessons: Social Organization in the Classroom*. Cambridge, Massachusetts: Harvard University Press.

——— (1981). 'Ethnography of bilingual education'. In H.T. Trueba, G.P. Guthrie & K.H. Au (eds), *Culture and the Bilingual Classroom: Studies in Classroom Ethnography*. Rowley, Massachusetts: Newbury House, 36–55.

Mercer, N., (1994). 'Neo-Vygotskyan theory and classroom education'. In B. Stierer & J. Maybin (eds) *Language, Literacy and Learning in Educational Practice*. Clevedon: Multilingual Matters, 92–110.

——— (2004). 'Sociocultural discourse analysis: Analysing classroom talk as a social mode of thinking'. *Journal of Applied Linguistics*, 1/2, 137–68.

Moll, L., C. Amanti, D. Neff & N. Gonzalez, (1992). 'Funds of knowledge for teaching: Using a qualitative approach to connect homes and classrooms'. *Theory into Practice*, 31/2, 132–41.

Phillipson, R., (1992). *Linguistic Imperialism*. Oxford: Oxford University Press.

Ramanathan, V., (2005). *The English-Vernacular Divide: Postcolonial Language Politics in Practice*. Clevedon, Avon: Multilingual Matters.

Ricento, T. L. & N. H. Hornberger, (1996). 'Unpeeling the onion: Language planning and policy and the ELT professional'. *TESOL Quarterly*, 30/3, 401–28.

Saxena, M., (2007). 'Multilingual and multicultural identities in Brunei Darussalam'. In A. Tsui & J. Tollefson (eds), *Language policy, Culture and Identity in Asian Contexts*. Mahwah, NJ: Lawrence Erlbaum, 143–62.

——— (2008). 'Ideology, policy and practice in bilingual classrooms: Brunei Darussalam'. In A. Creese & P. Martin (eds), *Encyclopedia of Language and Education*, Volume 9. Kluwer/Springer, 249–62.

——— (2009). 'Negotiating conflicting ideologies and linguistic otherness: Code-switching in English classrooms'. *English Teaching: Practice and Critique*, 8/2, 167–87.

——— (2010). 'Reconceptualising teachers' directive and supportive scaffolding in bilingual classrooms within the neo-Vygotskyan approach'. *Journal of Applied Linguistics and Professional Practice*, 7/2, 163–84.

Saxena, M. & M. Martin-Jones, (2013). 'Multilingual resources in classroom interaction: Ethnographic and discourse analytic perspective'. *Language and Education*, 27/4, 285–97.

Stroud, C., (2003). 'Postmodernist perspectives on local languages: African mother tongue education in times of globalization'. *International Journal of Bilingual Education and Bilingualism*, 6/1, 17–36.

CHAPTER 4

Teaching Hindi as a Less Commonly Taught Language in North America

RAJESH KUMAR

ABSTRACT

One of the most widely spoken language of the South Asian subcontinent and a prominent member of the Indo-Aryan family of languages, Hindi is truly prominent among less commonly taught languages of North America. In the recent years of the post-9/11 world, Hindi has been identified as a language of critical significance by the Department of Education, United States. With the emergence of a significant number of the immigrant community in different parts of the United States, several schools came up with Hindi teaching programmes in the early seventies. Though Hindi teaching programmes at several universities have become a significant part of the teaching schedule, the whole enterprise appears to be devoid of several required and supportive aspects of language teaching such as serious research, developing teaching materials, and teaching methods. In such a situation examining the teaching of Hindi as a truly less commonly taught language in non-western language programmes becomes imperative. We take a close look at several aspects of Hindi teaching including its engagement with sustainable teaching methodology, the target audience, and with innovative language teaching approaches.

INTRODUCTION

The nature and structure of society of North America has been described with several terms such as *melting pot* and *crystal bowl.*

The underlying fundamental reasoning appears quite obvious. People from almost all parts of the world live in the United States and a lot of them have called it home. Linguistically speaking, this has been quite an interesting zone too. Speakers of many languages from all parts of world live in different cities of North America. In short, socially and linguistically, United States of America is a multicultural and multilingual space. Learning one of the non-western languages (at times the term non-western has an arbitrary definition) is mandatory for college education. Depending upon global political situations/ developments, the Department of Education gives special attention to certain languages. Thus, the teaching of such languages is on the rise.

The history of Hindi teaching at American universities is not very old. It appears that the teaching of Hindi as a language was an informal exercise until the late 1960s. Around the same time, with the growing interest of researchers in India and Indian languages, Hindi teaching picked up. At one point, India meant only Hindi for many in America. Though, Hindi teaching never became a serious domain of teaching at any American university, it has continued its existence in many academic units of American universities. In post-9/11 America, Hindi has been identified as a language of critical significance by the Department of Education. In most parts of the world in general and in the United States in particular, the teaching of languages such as Arabic, Urdu, Persian, Pashto, and Hindi has been in focus in recent years.

In this paper, we will discuss teaching of Hindi as a critical or a less commonly taught non-western/ heritage/ foreign language in an American classroom. We will discuss the nature of the audience (i.e. composition of a 'Hindi' classroom) and some innovative approaches in its teaching.

Research in the Teaching of Language

A fair amount of work has been carried out concerning the teaching of less commonly taught non-western languages such as Arabic, Japanese, Korean (Kondo-Brown 2003) and Spanish (Valdés 2000).

Languages of South Asian origin (such as Urdu, Tamil, Telugu, Malayalam, Punjabi, Gujarati to name a few) in general and Hindi in particular have not been among such languages. Initially, most of the languages other than English and Spanish were termed as non-western languages. There appears to be clearly two groups among non-western languages. Latin, German, Italian, Russian, Chinese, Korean, and Japanese among others are major non-western languages in American schools. On the other hand, Arabic, Swahili, Pasto, Hindi, Urdu, Tamil, Telugu, Malayalam, Punjabi, are truly less commonly taught non-western languages. In an emerging trend, these languages have been attributed a new term—heritage languages. There have been two professional meetings on heritage languages; the first one was a national conference on heritage languages in 1999 in Long Beach, California and the other was the UCLA Language Steering Committee Meeting. On the one hand both meetings had similar outcomes where very less commonly taught languages were identified as heritage languages and were considered a 'national resource'. On the other hand, professionals working with these languages felt the need to identify the student population and consolidate students' profiles to design courses and materials that respect and recognise what learners bring to the class.

Most of the work on heritage language and heritage language learners came up following the United States Census of 1999 (Chevalier 2004). It shows 10% of the total population as foreign-born. It is not surprising that the statistics show this figure of foreign-born residents as the largest in United States history. Statistics show that in the 1990s Americans speaking a language other than English at home grew up by 47%. More than 150 languages other than English are spoken in the United States (Brecht and Ingold 2002). Such a change in statistics and eventually in demography, must attract the attention of policy makers and researchers. Nonetheless, Hindi does not appear to be receiving enough attention in the United States.

Disagreement exists among researchers and teachers about the term heritage language learners (Wiley 2001). While understanding the term heritage language learner, Carreira (2004) quotes the popular story of six blind men and an elephant[1]. Most researchers seem to agree with Fishman (2001) on the definition of heritage language. Heritage language includes any indigenous, colonial, and immigrant language which may or may not be a language regularly used in the home or in the community (Fishman 2001). Similarly, many seem to agree with Valdés' (2000) definition of a heritage language learner. According to her, a heritage speaker refers to 'a student who is raised in a home where a non-English language is spoken, who speaks or merely understands the heritage language, and who is to some extent bilingual in English and the heritage language' (Valdés 2000).

Focusing on Spanish learners, Valdés (2000) discusses the language characteristics of heritage learners. She talks about the ways in which bilingual heritage speakers develop skills in English and in the heritage language. She further discusses the challenges that the language pedagogy faces in the United States as well as the educators' attitude. Fishman (2001) and Wiley (2001) have highlighted issues in pedagogy as well. Wiley (2001) gives an account of national policies on heritage language education and maintenance. He observes a shift in the twentieth century in changing attitudes toward heritage speakers including 'promotion, accommodation, tolerance or suppression'.

Gambhir (2001) presents a clear situation of the Hindi teaching enterprise. He puts Hindi as 'Truly Less Commonly Taught Languages (TLCTLs)'. He contrasts it with the enrolment statistics of various languages. Needs, motivations and strengths of the learners of TLCTLs are well categorised in Gambhir (2001). Gambhir observes that the low enrolment in Hindi classes results in fewer class offerings at American universities. Subsequently, we get a class of students

[1] Six visually impaired men were describing an elephant to each other after having touched the elephant. Each of them came up with a description of the elephant based on the part he touched. They reached contradictory conclusions in the sense that they were not in agreement with each other. They resolved the issue when somebody who had seen the elephant described it to them. They realised that the integration of all their views as a composition in totality would give them a clearer picture.

with mixed proficiency in the target language. Among the challenges that the Hindi teaching enterprise is facing, Gambhir highlights, are non-native instructors, lack of appropriate teaching materials, teacher training, and informed methodology. The lack of research in teaching methodology and patterns of language acquisition in Hindi is worth mentioning here. In the next section, I would like to focus on the learner profile in Hindi classes.

Learner Profile in the Classroom

A steering committee meeting on heritage language teaching in 2000 at the UCLA concluded that heritage language acquisition begins at home as opposed to foreign language for which learning begins in a classroom. Such an observation puts Hindi in the list of heritage languages in the USA. In this section, I present the learner profile of Hindi in an American classroom. The teaching of Hindi as a language in American classroom does not have a long history. Until the early 1980s, Hindi was essentially a foreign language. We observe a systematic and continuous change in the learner type in classrooms. A considerable number of American-born South Asians have been coming for Hindi classes since the late nineties, and in recent years we find such students in majority in Hindi classes. This section discusses the composition of a typical Hindi class.

A typical Hindi classroom in most American schools comprises two groups, namely foreign language learners (FLL) and heritage language learners (HLL). Those who do not belong to the group of heritage language learners are foreign language learners who have come to learn Hindi. Heritage language learners bring some knowledge of language and culture to the classroom (+L, +C). On the basis of the empirical data from the classrooms in various Hindi teaching programmes, an observation helps us understand that foreign language learners do not bring any knowledge of language and culture to the classroom (–L, –C). Heritage language learners have had some Hindi or some other language of any language family, namely Indo-Aryan or Dravidian, prior to the Hindi class. The group of foreign language learners is assumed to have had no comparable opportunity before the Hindi class. It has widely been suggested that these two sub-groups of a Hindi class require separate attention.

Methodologically, the composition of a Hindi classroom with heritage language learners draws our attention in particular. The group of heritage language learners makes the classroom a totally heterogeneous group. Let's examine the internal nature of this group. Heritage language learners are of two types—strict heritage language learners (SHLL) and cognate heritage language learners (CHLL). Strict heritage language learners bring both language and culture (+L, +C) to the classroom. Among the cognate heritage language learners, we find two sub types—cognate heritage language learners (CHLL) and non-cognate heritage language learners (Non-CHLL). All types of heritage language learners have had one or the other Indo-Aryan language or Dravidian language in their background at home (i.e. outside the classroom). Students with Hindi in their background fall in the strict heritage language learners (SHLL) category, while students with any Indo-Aryan language other than Hindi, i.e. Bengali, Gujarati, Marathi, Konkani, etc. fall in the cognate heritage language learners category. Finally, students with Dravidian language (such as Tamil, Telugu, Kannada, and Malayalam) in their background fall in the non-cognate heritage language learners category. This classification of heritage language learners is purely based on the familiarity of the students with language and culture. In short, SHLLs bring both language and culture to the class (+L, +C). The situation is different with CHLLs i.e. ~L, +C. Note that it is not –L. However, Non-CHLLs come with no language but they do bring to the class familiarity with culture. Such is the variation of learners in a Hindi classroom. Foreign language learners are usually from English and Spanish backgrounds.

Innovation in Teaching Approach

From Skinner (1957) to Chomsky (1959, 1981, 1986), Piaget (1936) to Pinker (1994, 1997), and Hymes (1972, 1980) to Krashen (2003)—it has been established that a systematic understanding of the nature and structure of language has a lot to contribute to the teaching of language. Language teaching is a serious business. All aspects of teaching of a language (foreign language/ second language/ heritage language) require the following: a clear understanding of the target audience with their composition and motivation, a sound methodological grounding, and scientifically grounded teaching materials.

So far in this paper, we have established that Hindi is one of the truly less commonly taught languages in the USA and the audience (learners) in a Hindi classroom is very diverse. With such a wide range of learners in a Hindi classroom, aspirations and motivations of individual learners differ from one another and subsequently become a huge challenge for a professional teacher. Foreign language learners (FLLs) and Non-cognate heritage language learners (Non-CHLLs) fall in the same category in the sense that they have no knowledge of the written or spoken form of Hindi. The strict heritage language learners (SHLLs) and cognate heritage language learners (CHLLs) are familiar with at least spoken Hindi. Many from these two groups speak and understand some Hindi. They do not read or write Hindi. These observations come from answers for an initial survey form in a Hindi class at the University of Texas at Austin. In short, there is a clear pattern of two types of audience in Hindi classes. FLLs and Non-CHLLs constitute approximately 25% of an elementary Hindi class, whereas SHLLs and CHLLs constitute 75% of the class.

Having established such a pattern, I would like to evaluate teaching methodologies and teaching materials. There is a pattern in teaching methodology for elementary classes. An elementary class usually begins with an assisted instruction of the script across the board. This takes approximately 20% of the class time in a semester. Heritage learners perform well in learning this aspect as they learn faster than foreign language learners. On the other hand, once the learning of the script is taken care of, the heritage learner regresses, they make more mistakes than the foreign language learners do. FLLs seek more emphasis on the structure of language, whereas the HLLs (including Non-CHLLs) do not demand or prefer such an emphasis in the class. HLLs seek more information about the socio-cultural aspects of India. They want to be able to speak Hindi. From this point onwards, the teaching methodology is not to the satisfaction of all groups. Increasingly, it becomes difficult to meet the requirements of the two types of learners. Therefore, it is the demand of the times that proper screening of the learners takes place for effective instruction.

I would like to mention two experimental approaches in my Hindi classes at the University of Illinois at Urbana-Champaign and at the University of Texas at Austin. Kumar (2012, 2013) discusses parts of the outcome of such experiments. Cummins and Swain (1986) and Cummins (1993) convincingly show the correlations between multilingualism and scholastic achievements—higher the degree of multilingualism the greater the scholastic achievements and cognitive flexibility. Keeping the role of multilingualism in learning a language in mind, I did not stop or discourage learners from using any other language in the class. This eventually yielded positive results. Such results quickly get translated into desired learning. Keeping suggestions from Krashen (2003) in mind, the focus was always on the use of contextual, relevant, comprehensible and meaningful teaching materials for the learners. In yet another attempt to mix the two, Cummins and Swain (1986) and Krashen (2003), my feedback approach was not negative. At both the schools namely, University of Illinois and University of Texas mentioned above, one of the methods that I used as feedback for students was writing a short (two type-written pages) paper in Hindi on a topic of their choice. In the last seven weeks of a semester I helped the students with corrections twice. In the final week of the semester, students presented these papers in Hindi. And, finally these papers were collected and published in the form of a booklet. The final submission version of the paper was published without any further correction or editing. This was to keep originality intact as part of the positive feedback system.

Historically speaking, the Hindi teaching enterprise in the United State does not reveal a systematic effort in the preparation of teaching materials that follow from research in the study of language. In other words, the teaching of Hindi has been devoid of scientific (linguistic) research on several aspects of Hindi. Initially, the curricular framework was designed to deliver Hindi to foreign language learners. In one way or the other, elementary classes follow pattern drills for teaching with little meaningful input. It has been only a few years that the changing paradigm in learner type has been explored. Many Hindi teaching programmes have not responded to the need of a target audience in giving required attention to both groups yet. Similarly, teaching materials do not address learner-needs and contemporary contexts of learning situations of either of the two groups.

The proposed suggestions on the basis of successful experiments at two major Hindi teaching programmes in the USA namely, the University of Illinois and UT Austin are as follows. Teaching programmes require two separate tracks for two learner-types. It requires focus on the development of the teaching materials that incorporate interactive technologies to teach skills for spoken and written language in a manner that provides an understanding and appreciation of the cultural nuances of linguistic interaction with people of South Asia. Language learning must be embedded in the context of contemporary cultural settings with the goal of teaching the language and its use in the native cultural context with appropriate grammatical details. Materials must be grounded in the indigenous context and encourage multilingualism. Learners must negotiate meaning through interactional social context with knowledge of language use.

Conclusion

This paper focuses on the teaching of Hindi in American Universities, changing learner types and their aspirations in a Hindi language classroom. We evaluate teaching methodology and some innovative approaches for teaching. Learner type has changed from purely foreign language learners to largely heritage learners. This paper provides a description and classification of the heritage language learners in a Hindi class. Finally, this paper argues for the need of two separate tracks for teaching both types of learners as the requirements and expectations of the two types of learners are different. This paper also underlines the lack of specialised teaching materials and suggests that precautions must be exercised in designing such materials.

REFERENCES

Brecht, R. D. & C. W. Ingold, (2002). 'Tapping a national resource: Heritage languages in the United States'. *ERIC Digest* (*ERIC Clearinghouse on Languages and Linguistics, Washington, DC*), EDO-FL-02-2002.
http: //www.cal.org/resource-center/briefs-digests/digests/(offset)/105
Last accessed on 20 February 2014.

Carreira, M., (2004). 'Seeking explanatory adequacy: A dual approach to understanding the term "heritage language learner"'. *Heritage Language Journal*, 2/ 1, 1–25. http: //www.heritagelanguages.org/Journal.aspx
Last accessed on 05 February 2014.

Chevalier, J. F., (2004). 'Heritage language literacy: Theory and practice'. *Heritage Language Journal*, 2/ 1, 1–19.
http: //www.heritagelanguages.org/Journal.aspx
Last accessed on 05 February 2014.

Chomsky, N., (1959). 'Review of B. F. Skinner's verbal behavior'. *Language*, 35, 26–58.

——— (1981). 'Principles and parameters in syntactic theory'. In N. Hornstein & D. Lightfoot (eds), *Explanation in Linguistics: The Logical Problem of Language Acquisition*. London: Longman, 32–75.

——— (1986). *Knowledge of Language: Its Nature, Origin, and Use*. New York: Praeger.

Cummins, J., (1993). 'Bilingualism and second language learning'. *Annual Review of Applied Linguistics*, 13, 51–70.

Cummins, J. and M. Swain, (1986). *Bilingualism in Education: Aspects of Theory, Research, and Practice*. London: Longman.

Fishman, J., (2001). '300-plus years of heritage language education in the United States'. In J. K. Peyton, D. A. Ranard & S. McGinnis (eds), *Heritage Languages in America: Preserving a National Resource*. McHenry, IL: Delta Systems, 81–97.

Gambhir, S., (2001). 'Truly less commonly taught languages and heritage language learners in the United States'. In J. K. Peyton, D. A. Ranard & S. McGinnis (eds), *Heritage Languages in America: Preserving a National Resource*. McHenry, IL: Delta Systems, 207–228–97.

Hymes, D. H., (1972). 'On communicative competence'. In J. B. Pride & J. Holmes (eds), *Sociolinguistics: Selected Readings*. Harmondsworth: Penguin, 269–73.

——— (1980). *Language in Education: Ethnolinguistic Essays*. Washington, DC: Center for Applied Linguistics.

Kondo-Brown, K., (2003). 'Heritage language instruction for post-secondary students from immigration background'. *Heritage Language Journal*, 1/ 1, 1–25. http: //www.heritagelanguages.org/Journal.aspx Last accessed on 05 February 2014.

Krashen, S., (2003). *Explorations in Language Acquisition and Use*. Portsmouth: Heinemann.

Kumar, R., (2012). 'Multilinguality and English: Choice of language for education in India'. *FORTELL*, 25, 24–26.

——— (2013). 'Linguistic analyses: Implications for language teaching'. *Language and Language Teaching*, 1/ 2, 22–26.

Piaget, J., (1936). *Origins of Intelligence in the Child*. London: Routledge and Kegan Paul.

Pinker, S., (1994). *The Language Instinct*. New York: Harper Perennial Modern Classics.

——— (1997). *How the Mind Works*. New York: WW Norton and Company.

Skinner, B. F., (1957). *Verbal Behaviour*. New York: Appleton-Century-Crofts.

Valdés, G., (2000). 'Spanish for native speakers'. In N. Anderson (ed.), *The American Association of Teachers of Spanish and Portuguese (AATSP) Development Series: Handbook for Teachers K-16*, Orlando, FL: Harcourt College Publishers, 1–20.

Wiley, T. G., (2001). 'On defining heritage languages and their speakers'. In J. K. Peyton, D. A. Ranard and S. McGinnis (eds), *Heritage Languages in America: Preserving a National Resource*, McHenry, IL: Delta Systems, 29–36.

CHAPTER 5

Linguistic and Cultural Diversity and Language Teaching—with a Specific Focus on the Teaching of Reading and Writing to Young Learners

KEERTI JAYARAM

ABSTRACT

Recent research has highlighted that the first one or two years in school are extremely important for facilitating a successful transition from home to school, especially for those young learners who are from diverse social, cultural and linguistic backgrounds and are actively encountering print for the first time when they enter school. Further, the Emergent Literacy perspective has emphasised that unless children acquire literate behaviours through using print and interacting with others within their social environments, they are often unable to go beyond a mechanical and incomplete mastery of the written code.

Based on the above thinking this paper will present the field based experience and insights arrived over the past six years through work undertaken within the Organisation Early Literacy Project (OELP). OELP may be viewed as an exploratory search for ways in which issues of diversity and home-school transitions can be addressed meaningfully within mainstream classrooms for beginning school-goers who are from marginalised home backgrounds. This project has aimed to equip these young learners with strong foundations for meaningful and efficient reading and writing in Hindi. The conceptualisations of early literacy in the OELP intervention have been viewed within an overarching theoretical framework which positions itself within socio-cultural and constructivist perspectives, which privilege meaning over mechanical skills; with early literacy seen much more in terms of socio-cultural and historical processes within which individual internal cognitive and linguistic development occurs. An attempt has been made within this project to recognise the importance of addressing the special learning needs of children who come from non-literate homes and diverse backgrounds.

OELP interventions have three main components. These are:

1. *Planned methods for building non-threatening, active and responsive reading and writing classroom environments, as a critical component of classroom practice. These are monitored through clearly identified indicators.*
2. *A systematic approach for building script knowledge which equips children to use the script actively and meaningfully to construct the written forms of their own spoken language.*
3. *A systematic programme for engaging children with children's literature, which aims to equip young beginning level learners to become efficient and involved readers and writers.*

This paper will also attempt to locate ELP within the existing larger context of Emergent and Early Literacy Programmes in the Indian context.

THE CONTEXT

Multiculturalism and multilingualism have increasingly come to occupy centre stage within the mainstream discourse on quality education. This is reflected within current literature on education, as well as through policy documents which view linguistic and cultural diversity as intrinsic attributes of human society and strive to include these as resources that can enrich and enhance learning situations including school classrooms. Almost a decade ago Nadine Dutcher (2004), in an extensive review of on-going programmes in thirteen countries suggested that the reviewed programmes have been successful in some ways in expanding educational opportunity in their linguistically diverse societies. Many of the reviewed countries have initiated innovative programmes that begin instruction in the children's first language, bridging successfully to a second language that is a language of wider communication.

Children in these programmes have the opportunity to develop their cognitive skills, including reading and writing, through their first language while acquiring the basis for learning the second language. These are efforts to ensure that the children are culturally rich and secure in their identity within their own group; they are linguistically competent and gain the ability to participate in the wider society within and outside their countries.

Within the Indian context the stage was set with the National Curriculum Framework (2005), which has strongly and convincingly upheld the argument for linguistic and cultural diversity to be viewed as resources that enrich and enhance classroom practice. The more recent Right of Children to Free and Compulsory Education Act (2009) has further emphasised that the language of instructions should be the mother tongue to the extent possible, as this will enable the child to learn in her/ his own socio-linguistic context. Within a vast body of work in the field of education which addresses linguistic and cultural diversity within the Indian education context, there is a long cherished promise of a better, freer and more just society which has engaged the educational imagination in recent years.

Facilitating Natural Learning Processes of Learning

As adults we are often in danger of forgetting just how abstract and symbolic much of what we present to children in school really is. Margaret Donaldson (1978) in her seminal work draws attention to the fact that it is important to understand that children's thinking is not inferior to adults, but rather that it is different in form and experience. Their thinking is embedded in their experience. This experience becomes the context that provides meaning for them, whereas much of school activity is divorced from contexts in which children see real meaning and purpose. Children bring to the school their real world experience and knowledge. They also bring their imaginations, curiosities and natural inclinations to be purposefully engaged. There is a need to ensure that a variety of experiences which support children's natural ways of learning become available to children inside classrooms, particularly in the early school years. Recent studies have shown that the closer the match between home and community-based learning practices and school-based practices within the early years of schooling; the more likely it is that children will build strong foundations for meaningful learning.

Some Relevant Theoretical Perspectives

Vygotsky (1978) considered a child's development to be an inherently social process. An important element highlighted by Vygotsky is that even a young child has a symbolic life which is rich and saturated with meaning and that it is essentially through this that a child mediates with the world. For Vygotsky, development occurs when the child internalises from the social sphere. In other words a young child is seen as actively constructing her symbolic inner world. He argues that the emergence of the symbolic life is not a 'natural' outcome of some pre-determined genetic timetable, but is rather the result of internalisation or socialisation from the social/inter-personal sphere. Both the structure and content of a child's inner world are shaped by the inter-personal interactions that a child finds herself in.

Building further on Vygotsky's ideas, researchers of language development and early literacy, who view literacy learning as meaning-making constructions rather than learning of letter-sound relationships, have demonstrated that literacy learning begins long before formal instruction in school (Wells 1986, Clay 2001). The Emergent Literacy perspective also emphasises that it is through active participation and exposure to a variety of informal reading and writing and meaning making experiences that constitute language experiences at home, that very young children begin to make meaningful relationships with different forms of reading and writing much before they enter school. Literature borne out of the field of Emergent Literacy points out that very young learners generate a network of competencies and strategies out of early reading experiences in their homes which power subsequent independent literacy learning. Such children come better equipped to deal with school learning than their peers who are encountering print for the first time when they enter school. These research findings have implications for the literacy acquisition of children who do not have such early literacy exposure (Teale and Sulzby 1986).

Some of this thinking is reflected within the vast body of multidisciplinary and ethnographic research on 'reading' and 'literacy' from the eighties and nineties which witnessed a shift towards socio-cultural, socio-linguistic and anthropological perspectives. This body of work began to overshadow the earlier debates on approaches to reading (see Pearson 2001). Shirley Brice Heath (1983), in her classic ethnographic study, highlights the complex processes through which a child learns the social rules of meaning at home and then extends these rules to the texts encountered in schools. Heath demonstrated how children from different communities were differentially prepared for schooling that promoted and privileged only middle-class ways of using language. She made an argument for researchers and teachers to identify what kind of literacy was valued in schools, and the ways in which children from diverse socio-cultural and linguistic backgrounds needed to be adequately equipped for school success.

Issues of Equity and Difference

Addressing issues of diversity in the classroom implies engagement with the more complex underlying issues of discontinuities between the children's home languages and the language of school. Inherent within such discontinuities are issues related to the so called standard and non-standard languages and dominant and minority cultures practice. Lisa Delpit (1998), in a powerful essay titled 'The silenced dialogue: Power and pedagogy in educating other people's children' elaborates that for her the dilemma of educating 'black' children in America is not one of addressing instructional methodology, but rather one communicating across cultures and of addressing the more fundamental issue of power; of whose voice gets to be heard in determining what is best for children from underprivileged groups, as well as in the need to create space within the mainstream for alternative cultural codes. Brian Street (2003) and the New Literacy Studies build this argument further by claiming that the act of reading in itself is not an autonomous and neutral cognitive activity, but is in fact a social and cultural practice which is contested in terms of power. In other words, hidden within the act of reading are issues of identity and power.

As a practitioner I have found these concerns resonating inside the OELP classrooms. These classrooms appeared to us to be microcosmic reflections of the dynamics within the larger stratified Indian society. Through our field work, we have on several occasions experienced the fact that access to school does not necessarily translate into school inclusion, and social or linguistic difference can in fact lead to situations of exclusion within classroom transactions. There are instances when learners from diverse groups are viewed in terms of being deficit. The likelihood of such instances gets heightened in cases where there is a distinct social distance between the teacher and the learner. We realised that for many young school-goers the experience of early schooling was in fact one of facing rejection and acquiring a low self-esteem. Perhaps this is the reason why children from socially marginalised communities were often found to be silent spectators in the classroom, and it took a fair amount of sensitive handling and a concerted effort on our part to motivate them to participate in the class activity. Inclusion of all children within the classroom processes thus became an area of concern for us.

Agnihotri (2007) makes the compelling point that languages associated with power can no longer be allowed to exploit the speakers of languages that are spoken by the underprivileged. He calls for a more comprehensive and socio-linguistically situated education which looks 'for a society that ensures autonomy of mind and reflection and of care and respect for others.' Perhaps one of the biggest challenges facing today's teachers and teacher educators' revolves around the ways in which schools can be made to work effectively and equitably for all learners in ever more diverse classrooms which exist within an increasingly global and technologically driven world

The Experience of the Organisation for Early Literacy Promotion (OELP)

OELP was located within some of the above thinking and concerns. It developed organically as an exploratory search for ways of building strong foundations for meaningful reading and writing, for children from diverse and underprivileged backgrounds who may not have support or opportunities for actively engaging with reading and writing in their homes or social worlds. The interventions within OELP grew organically through sustained engagement inside resource poor classrooms. This project was born out of several years of earlier experience with young children in government schools in Delhi. Many of these children were reading and writing mechanically and were unable to make any sense of what they read. Most of these classrooms had seemed to be fairly sterile places within which children were expected to play the passive roles of receivers of knowledge which their teacher transmitted to them as the content of a predetermined syllabus. A few classrooms were even threatening and hostile, especially for children from evidently marginalised groups. Within this context the first challenge was to make the classroom an accepting and engaging learning space for young learners so that each child feels a sense of belonging and is willing to engage, experiment and take risks as a part of an active process of learning and growing.

Our work began in classes 1, 2 and 3 in six Municipal Corporation (MCD) Schools in Delhi, and was implemented for one year, from July 2006. The children who attend these schools are mostly children of migrant, daily wage workers, from different parts of the country. After a year of intensive and sustained work inside classrooms within this urban context, this exploratory search was relocated to schools in the drought prone area of rural Rajasthan. In this new location, we began work inside classrooms in government primary schools, as well as, in non-formal centres which aim to provide support to children who have not survived formal school and have 'dropped out', or children who are unable to attend school in the day. This work in rural Rajasthan is still in process.

Conceptualisation of the OELP Interventions

OELP evolved through an organic process of intensive and sustained engagement inside classrooms which was supplemented by insights from available literature. We located ourselves within the Balanced Approach with:

a) planned opportunities for building and strengthening foundations for sustained and meaningful involvement with reading and writing which included children's literature; and
b) a structured programme for building core literacy skills for the linguistic processes of developing phonological awareness as well as the cognitive processes for meaning making.

As mentioned earlier, through our engagement inside classrooms for beginners we had discovered that home-based early reading and writing experiences had not been available to the group of children that we were working with. Classroom-based individual reading observations made it apparent that the transition from the spoken language at home to the print culture of the classroom was in fact pretty daunting for many of these young learners. They were struggling through texts that made no sense to them. Most children were sounding out words in fragmented, disconnected and tedious ways. It became clear to us that the children we were working with are at a disadvantage when compared with their more middle-class peers who enter a school equipped with the foundation of print concepts which they have picked up through every day interactions during their early years at home. The children within these OELP classrooms slipped very quickly, into mechanical drills and rote memorisation. It was frustrating to discover that with a gap of even a few days in the school calendar they would forget all that they had learned and went right back to square one.

We soon realised that many of these children did not view reading and writing as a personally meaningful processes. Most of them looked at reading and writing as 'something to do with school.' Our first challenge therefore was to find ways to help such children to make personal connections with written words. We wanted these children to realise that reading and writing has something to do with 'them.' In the same ways as with spoken language, they can express their words, ideas, feeling and imaginations through written forms. We believed that it was important for these children to experience the processes of reading and writing as something meaningful. Underlying this belief was our need to acknowledge each learner as a productive and unique member of the class.

As we groped our way through unchartered waters, we were influenced by the distinction put forth by McNaughton (1995) who had distinguished between two possible complementary learning systems in the classroom, namely:

a) the tutorial system or the learning interaction between the adult teacher and the child learners, and
b) the personal learning system of an individual child.

Based on this thinking we discovered the value in acknowledging the need for both learning systems to coexist in distinct, yet mutually supportive ways within classrooms. This meant that in addition to teacher initiated learning interactions based on the formal curriculum, the children were encouraged to bring in and share their real world and language experiences inside the classroom. We now felt the need to consciously plan for both learning systems. Within OELP, this led to viewing the classroom as a social setting which offers the possibility for learning based on a variety of authentic social practices. The basic assumption being that young learners will acquire and strengthen their competencies in written language and scientific concepts, in the same ways as they do for their spoken language and everyday concepts i.e., through the purposeful and meaningful usage and through active engagement with their immediate social and physical environment. This vision led us to view the walls of the classroom as a buffer zone between the children's real worlds outside the classroom and the world that exists inside the classroom.

We began by placing attractive name charts on the walls. The children's excitement was palpable. These generated a number of meaningful activities based on the written forms of the children's names. Names charts, name cards, drawings and name games were gradually included. Slowly, these got extended to include the names of family members, friends and so on. There were animated conversations and a host of activities that grew in organic ways. This gave the children a sense of acceptance and a heightened sense of self and at the same time engaged them in making meaningful connections with written letters and sounds. Gradually words, stories, poems appeared in specially demarcated spaces. Perhaps it's important to point out that these displayed texts were negotiated. Thus words in the word wall were the children's words. Slowly a whole range of reading and writing activities based on the children's experience evolved and found spaces on the walls of the classrooms.

Three-pronged Approach

It is important to explain that within OELP a systematic programme for building script knowledge in meaningful ways also grew side by side. Slowly a three-pronged approach developed which focused on:

a) developing non-threatening and active classroom learning environments
b) building script knowledge in meaningful ways. This included a focus on core skills, i.e. linguistic skills for building phonological awareness and the cognitive skills for meaning construction, and
c) building a love for books and reading through planned engagement with children's literature.

Once the children are equipped with script knowledge they are encouraged to actively construct the written forms of their spoken language. Predetermined word lists are not used, but the children are encouraged to engage with word walls, poem posters, riddles, storybooks and a variety of displayed texts.

Building Relationships

'Quality' in early education has often been defined in terms of adult-child ratios, group size, physical facilities, and, more recently, cognitively oriented curriculum. Recent work undertaken at the Center on the Developing Child at Harvard University (2004) has emphasised the need to widen this discourse to include the responsiveness and sensitivity of the classroom learning environment to the varied needs of individual children. This work has emphasised that young children experience their world as an environment of relationships, and these relationships affect virtually all aspects of their development—intellectual, social, emotional, physical, behavioural, and moral. There are significant implications of this body of work on the importance of building responsive classroom. Young learner classrooms need to be designed to provide a sensitive, caring and stimulating environment to engage learners from diverse backgrounds in active and meaningful ways that enhance their learning.

Within OELP we found that setting up such facilitative and interactive classroom learning environments does not have to be resource intensive. We also experienced the incidental impact that such environments have on the role of the teacher, which gradually shifts from one of a transmitter of knowledge to one of an active co-traveller.

Responsive Teachers

A large number of teachers have been locked into centralised instructional and assessment practices which have often not been effective in informing classroom processes and practice; especially within situations of diversity. Their distanced objectivity tends to make them mechanical and ineffective for addressing the complexity of classroom realities. Our experience within OELP suggests that teachers need to be able to take a proactive professional stance towards teaching and negotiating learning processes within classrooms that honour learner diversity. Proactive teachers need to feel in charge of the learning environment and of the learning processes for each child. It is important for teachers to be adequately equipped for engaging with and managing classroom complexities and diversity through capacity building programmes which are grounded within classroom realities.

Some facilitating features are:

- Use of children's home language in the classroom and plenty of opportunity for usage and enrichment of oral language and active listening in the classroom.

- Use of daily planned read-aloud sessions and other pedagogies for vocabulary development and building reading comprehension to support young learners to make a meaningful shift from spoken to written forms of language.
- Setting up interactive wall spaces in the classrooms such as attractive name charts; word walls; interactive calendars; poem corner; children's writing and drawing corner; reading corner etc. All these are not resource intensive, but they provide spaces in the classroom which engage children in with a variety of written text in natural and purposeful ways.
- Provision of space and material for free writing, drawing and other forms of expression.
- Seating arrangements that facilitate peer learning and interactive group work.
- Collaborative work through which meanings can be negotiated and shared meanings arrived at. For example through games based on the word wall, through extensions of displayed poems, through shared writings, through projects based on the interests and concerns of the learners and through the worlds of stories.
- Most importantly, shifting the focus of assessment from an assessment of learner outcomes to an assessment of learner needs and then monitoring those needs and addressing them through a variety of classroom based learning strategies.

Designing for Success

The attainment of equal opportunity for all children requires that each child experiences school as a positive leaning experience. This reinforces the need to create culturally and linguistically sensitive and non-threatening classrooms for learning environments which allow space and opportunity for learners to follow their own learning trajectories within some broadly defined learning parameters. The first one or two years in school are important for facilitating a successful transition from home to school for young learners. If a young child's home language and the world that it encompasses, does not find acceptance within the classroom, it is unlikely that she will participate meaningfully in the classroom processes; instead it is more likely that the child will internalise rejection, and adopt the role of a benign spectator or non-participant who does not want to risk failure (Purcell-Gates 1995).

The goal of every teacher needs to be the development of instructional programmes and learning environments that are designed to prevent failure and increase opportunity for success for each child. This requires norms within classroom transactions and learning processes that permit diverse and multiple usages and interpretations so that they provide inclusive access to learning while at the same time catering to the diverse learning needs of individual children in the classroom.

References

Agnihotri, R. K., (2007). 'Towards a pedagogical paradigm rooted in multilinguality'. *International Multilingual Research Journal*, 1/2, Mahwah, NJ: Lawrence Erlbaum Associates Inc. 1–10.

Clay, M. M., (2001). *Change Over Time in Children's Literacy Development*. Portsmouth, NH: Heinemann, 224.

Delpit, L. D., (1998). 'The silenced dialogue: Power and pedagogy in educating other people's children'. *Harvard Education Review*, 59/ 3, 208–98.

Donaldson, M., (1978). *Children's Minds*. Glasgow: Fontana.

Dutcher, N., (2004). 'Expanding educational opportunity in educationally diverse societies'. Washington DC: Center for Applied Linguistics. http: //www.cal.org/resources/pubs/fordreport_040501.pdf Last accessed on 18 November 2016.

Heath, S. B., (1983). *Ways with Words: Language, Life, and Work in Communities and Classrooms*. New York: Cambridge University Press.

McNaughton. S., (1995). In J. Smith & W. Elley (1997). *How Children Learn to Write*, London: Paul Chapman Publishing Ltd: 22–24

National Scientific Council on the Developing Child. (2004). *Young Children Develop in an Environment of Relationships.* Working Paper No. 1. http: //www.developingchild.net Last accessed on 12 August 2016.

Pearson, D., (2001). 'Reading in the twentieth century'. CIERA Archive #01–08 http: //www.ciera.org/ library/archive/2001-08/0108pd Last accessed on 12 August 2016.

Purcell-Gates, V., (1995). *Other People's Words: The Cycle of Low Literacy.* Cambridge, MA: Harvard University Press.

Street, B.V., (2003). 'What's new in new literacy studies? Critical approaches to literacy in theory and practice'. *Current Issues in Comparative Education*, 5/ 2, 77–91.

Teale, W. H. and E. Sulzby, (eds), (1986). *Emergent Literacy: Writing and Reading,* Norwood, NJ: Ablex.

Vygotsky, L., (1978). *Mind and Society: The Development of Higher Psychological Processes.* In M. Cole, V. John-Steiner, S. Scribner, and E. Souberman (eds), Cambridge, MA: Harvard University Press.

Wells, G., (1986). *The Meaning Makers: Children Learning Language and Using Language to Learn.* Portsmouth, NH: Heinemann Educational Books.

CHAPTER 6

Teaching Language and Achieving Literacy: Interfering with Learning, or Guiding It?

R. AMRITAVALLI

ABSTRACT

In literacy and language development, a truly learner-centred approach is one that understands the natural ways in which the mind learns language and develops literacy skills, and tries to aid this process through teaching and socialisation. In the arena of education, contemporary theory and folk wisdom (a form of compassionate common sense developed through observation and generalisation) must coexist with the aim of benefiting the learner. In the absence of these, learners are totally alienated from learning within the school. I draw on anecdotal evidence to illustrate how schooling is becoming increasingly alienated from the process of learning, and appeal for a synergy between teaching and cognitive science to inform the process of teacher-formation in society.

THE WHY AND THE HOW OF TEACHING READING

It is now acknowledged that children are natural language learners. They come to school with an oral knowledge of their home languages. For these languages, schooling concerns itself with literacy—the reading skill. In India, many children also learn a new language in school at the same time as they learn to read it. This language may be English, but it may also be an Indian language other than the child's home language(s).

I have discussed elsewhere (Amritavalli 2012) what the aim should be of 'teaching reading': to make a child into a reader. I shall in this paper focus on how to achieve this aim: how to teach reading in such a way as to turn children into readers.

'Reading readiness' and a 'print saturated' environment

Let me begin by sharing an anecdote about a response to our efforts to make child-friendly, attractive textbooks for beginning readers, not only in English but in other languages taught at school. Textbook writers and materials producers nowadays try to include pictures or illustrations, and large and readable print, with more 'white space' on the page. One response has been that pictures 'distract' the child from learning to read. A prominent bookseller told me that parents, too, prefer to buy books for their children where the 'page is full' of text. Such books are seen as better 'value for money' than a page which looks, for example, like this one:

The Carpenter
Ramu is a carpenter.
He makes a chair.
He makes a chair for me.
Ramu the carpenter is my father.

It appears that we want to 'saturate' or completely fill the child's book with all the print that it can hold. Now children in a 'print saturated' environment (as it is sometimes called) do seem to learn to read more easily, or more naturally, than other children. They seem to know what reading means before they come to school. They are said to have 'reading readiness'. But the kind of 'print saturation' that helps a child to become a reader is quite different from the idea that the more words per page, the better the book; or that pictures will distract the child's attention from letters and words.

Children go from a holistic perception of an illegible page of writing which nevertheless holds some meaning for them, to the details of words and letters. So while the alphabet, words and letters are important for a child to learn to read, these elements of print do not psychologically 'come before' the message.

A pre-literate child can get some meaning from a picture that is given along with printed words. If an adult reads out the words that 'tell the story', over time, the child naturally learns to pay attention to and read the words instead of just looking at the picture. Anyone who has regularly read stories out to children (two to five-year-olds) to amuse them will have experienced this. So story reading with children, a natural and pleasurable shared experience in child-rearing, is also a vital educational experience. There are teachers who, beginning with pre-school, help children to read and enjoy stories throughout their growing years. These teachers may not always be able to explain or justify what they are doing, but their pupils learn to read and write well, and remember their reading experiences with pleasure.

What is a 'print saturated' environment?

Children get the idea of what reading is from an idea of the purposes that reading serves. A 'print saturated' environment is one where the child sees the written language used every day, in a most normal and natural way, in the lives of the people she lives with. If you are reading this article, you probably come from a home where—

- you get a newspaper, magazines, pamphlets and so on every day;
- you make little notes of things to remember to buy, or to do;
- you have a calendar on the wall.

You could probably add many more things to this list of how we interact with written language or print in our daily lives. Now if we are fairly busy, we may quickly glance at the headlines in the morning; read just an item or two that interests us in the newspaper or magazine, or glance at the calendar momentarily to plan our day, week or month. The lists we make of things to do or to buy would be short and to the point. That is, the adult in a 'print saturated' environment does not always spend forty continuous minutes reading or writing, as a child in class is required to do. In what sense is her world 'print saturated'?

It is so in the sense that an adult naturally, spontaneously, turns to written language—reading and writing—to support her everyday activities. She might key-in a reminder on her cell phone. She might circle a date on a calendar. She might read a notice on the apartment's bulletin board, or take a list when she goes shopping. But every time she uses writing or reading like this, in however small a way, she models for the child the uses of literacy in our lives.

Literacy for Organising Daily Lives

This is the aspect of literacy that we try to model in the classroom by asking children to write the date on the blackboard, write down their names or addresses on their books and in the school registers, take down from the blackboard or through dictation notices to themselves or to their parents (about homework, school events, and so on), or make timetables and charts for their classroom duties or attendance. A moment's reflection will tell us that children enjoy these activities. They do not think of them as a chore or drudgery, but rather as a privilege. A moment's reflection will also tell us that we do not think of these as teaching and learning activities, but as time taken away from teaching the textbook.

Perhaps this is because of our lack of confidence in ourselves as teachers, and in the learning abilities of children. The immigrant American humourist Groucho Marx is famously said to have remarked that 'he would never join any club that would have him'. Clubs are places of privilege. Groucho is laughing at himself (poking fun at his own lack of confidence); he paradoxically defines any club that would admit such an ordinary person such as himself as 'a club not worth joining' (a not-so-special place). It appears that teachers similarly think that anything that their pupils learn to do easily or joyfully is not serious enough to be considered 'teaching and learning'.

Literacy for recording information and emotion

Children are very sensitive to the use of written language for communicating emotions or information. When a child sees a doctor write out a prescription, the chances are that she will play 'doctor' by writing out prescriptions (as she sometimes plays 'teacher'); especially if going to the doctor has been a fairly difficult or stressful experience for her. Children come to terms with their experiences by re-enacting them; if print has been a part of that experience it will be included in the re-enactment. You might want to reflect if you have seen any children write out detailed instructions to others, in the way they have seen their parents do. I recall children of an earlier era learning to look up telephone directories and making phone calls to order things; or writing out instructions to the newspaper boy during the holidays ('No newspaper until …'). I also recall eight-year-olds writing post cards to each other, just to see for themselves if the postman would deliver their letters! With a little cooperation from persons outside school, such simple, playful activities suitable to this day and age can easily be planned at least two or three times during a school year.

Literacy for the imagination: Iconic word recognition

Finally, the most important purpose of literacy is to fire the imagination. The obvious example is story reading, mentioned at the outset. Later, for a child who reads easily and well, even the sciences will tell stories—stories about the world around us. To begin with, though, we read out stories to the child, and read stories with the child. How does this promote literacy?

First of all, the child will want to learn to read, once she realises that reading unlocks a treasure house (of stories). When we read a story with a child, she realises that spoken words are somehow captured in writing. In the beginning, she might think of a whole word as having a corresponding printed shape. This is called 'iconic' recognition, where a written word is like a picture of a spoken word. This is the way we all recognise the logos of companies or products. Children begin to recognise words iconically as early as at the age of two: such as the label of a favourite drink or biscuit. During story reading with an adult, a child may begin to look for and iconically recognise the name of a favourite character (such as Ali Baba), or words that are important in the story: such as a magic spell, 'Open sesame'.

At this stage, a child may also do 'iconic writing'. Three- or four-year-old children from literate homes may have learnt to write their names, and ask for help to write a sister's or friend's name, if they wish to address a greeting card to the person.

Knowing the Alphabet: Letter and Word Recognition

As a teacher, you know that iconic recognition is not enough for the child to become a reader. Our languages are alphabetic languages; they are not pictographic or ideographic languages. To learn to read is to learn that letters stand for sounds. If we can use the 'alphabetic principle' that letters map systematically into sounds, we can also read and write unknown words. (Yes, there are irregular words, just as there are irregular rules of grammar for the past tense of verbs, or the plurals of nouns. Such irregularities are not enough for us to throw away the rule.) And indeed, a robust finding of reading research is that children who know their letter names reliably and automatically, become good readers.

Letter recognition and letter-to-sound mapping can be taught in a fun way, not just out of an alphabet and word book. We can ask children which of their classmates have names starting with a particular letter, to draw their attention to the kinds of sounds that the letter spells out. We can write down new but familiar names on the board and let them speak out the name from the spelling. I have done this in class II of a municipal school. I wrote on the board 'My name is Amrit'. A brief period of confusion and hesitation was followed by a chorus of 'A-M-am—Amrit!'

SOUNDS, RHYMES AND WORD ATTACK SKILLS

Learning to decode print becomes enjoyable and memorable in the context of action songs, poems and rhymes. Spelling-to-sound decoding is learnt best when children are taught 'nursery rhymes', as the researcher Usha Goswami has shown. The 'arbitrariness' or irregularity of English spelling is reduced by about half, when the spelling of 'the part that rhymes' is taken as a unit. Compare the sound and the spelling in the word columns below. What regularity do you see?

it	kite	hot	dote	at	ate
pit	bite	not	note	sat	late
sit	site	rot	rote	cat	gate
bit	mite	lot	tote	mat	rate

We pronounce the letters 'i,' 'o' or 'a' in a different way when a letter 'e' occurs at the end of the word. A child's way, an easy way, of understanding this is: *it*, *at*, *ot* are pronounced differently than *ite*, *ate*, and *ote*. This is a 'modified phonic approach'. It allows us to see that words that rhyme may also share a spelling. (Of course, they need not: words pairs like *rite* and *right*, *site* and *sight*, are called 'pure rhymes'. But now the child learns that the spelling sequences *ite* and *ight* have the same pronunciation.)

Goswami's work shows that children learn English letter-to-sound mapping better by paying attention to rhyme than to alliteration (words that begin with the same sound). It is better to teach word patterns like *bite*, *kite*, *site*, than *bat*, *bit*, *bet*, *but*. In the first set, we can easily see the spelling and sound pattern */b/ – /ite/*, */k/ – /ite/*, and */s/ – /ite/*. It is more difficult to see the spelling and sound pattern */b/ – /at/*, */b/ – /it/*, */b/ – /et/*, and */b/ – /ut/*. (Alliteration also helps reading, but at a later stage.)

When children learn spelling along with rhyme, they see that groups of letters can have a sound; so they learn to read words as letter groups, rather than haltingly, letter by letter. Children also recall words better when they pay attention to rhyme. I have described how first generation learners preparing for a class 7 examination read a poem *The Swing* (Amritavalli 2007). There was a question in the book: 'Find words that rhyme with *swing*.' The students remembered that in their textbook, there was a lesson on the hovercraft, with the sentence 'It can fly but it has no wings'. They remembered the word *wing* because it rhymes with *swing*!

Learners at the initial stages of language learning are much more sensitive to such similarities in sound than we are. They can also get more confused by such similarities. A class of adult foreign learners to whom I gave a task of reading library rules, found this instruction confusing: 'If you return a book late, you must pay a fine'. They knew the phrase 'How are you? Fine, thank you'. A colleague of mine who teaches French recalls that a French learner of English used to confuse *kitchen*, *chicken*, and *keychain*! I knew a learner who confused *onion* and *anyone*. These 'mistakes' are evidences that the mind is processing and trying to remember language. They are not anything for the learner to be ashamed of, or for the teacher to worry about. If they happened in 'real life' outside the classroom, we would laugh them off while we gently corrected them.

Decoding and Meaningful Reading need to go Together

Our schools are occupied in teaching decoding; what they neglect is meaningful reading. Knowing the alphabet is 'necessary, but not sufficient' to become a reader. According to Adams (1990: 21), the earliest method of reading instruction, till the 1850s, was to teach the alphabet with the help of key words (*G is for grass*), then to practise reading simple words, and exercises in spelling. In those days, children read mainly the holy books; not much else was available to read. A rigorous exercise in the comparison of reading programmes in the 1960s suggested that children taught with a combination of phonics instruction (emphasising systematic letter-sound correspondences) and considerable emphasis on connected reading and meaning outperformed those taught by either one of those methods. 'An early opportunity to do meaningful connected reading in addition to learning how to decode is needed to integrate both abilities' (Adams 1990: 45).

A beginning textbook today may have picture pages with poems and stories for the teacher to read out to the children, and activities to enjoy with them. The idea is that meaningful oral language activity, along with the printed text, is a foundation for the reading skill. The feedback from very experienced primary school teachers is that such textbooks cannot be used: 'The children can't read this; they don't even know their alphabet.'

The intention of these textbooks is to create in school the same 'reading rich' environment that some children have at home, that gives them an indefinable advantage when they come to school. There is no need for the child in class 1 to read every word in a textbook that has stories and poems. There is no need for children to not enjoy poems and stories until they have 'learnt their A-B-C-D'. The teacher can—by all means—teach the letters: their names, and their sounds, along with telling stories and poems. A whole textbook may not be needed for teaching letters; a simple alphabet chart will do the job. But to teach a five-year old only that *A is for apple*, is to convince her that reading is not of any use or interest for her.

What about comprehension? Here again, it is not useful to insist on what we think should be understood, but to sympathetically pay attention to what a child understands. In the municipal school I have spoken of, in class 2, the teacher had put some sentences up on the board from a story 'The magic pot'. I asked the children in Hindi, "Can you find a word on the board that means *dauRna* ('run')?" I expected them to point to the word 'run.' But the first answer was from a child who pointed out the word 'follow'. Was his answer right or wrong?

I accepted his answer, because when you think about it, 'follow' means 'to go after'. In that story, it could well have meant 'to run after' rather than 'to walk after' (the porridge was following someone, I think). So the child was learning as a group, words with the shared meaning of *go*. We know that babies may say 'doggie' for any four-legged animal. For the class 2 child, a group of movement-words were associated with the word 'run.'

What Research and Experience Tell Us

Even in children's home languages, reading is served better when the child is allowed to develop its vocabulary and imagination by playing games or telling stories (Nag and Snowling 2011). Children learn English better when they listen to and read stories along with the teacher (Jangid and Amritavalli 2011). There are autobiographical accounts of learning English through story-reading (Mangubhai 2011). For the interested teacher, a good introduction to the teaching of reading is Adams (1990). For the technologically comfortable teacher, the internet is a source of tips and anecdotes about how to teach reading, rhymes, poems and songs for the classroom.

Most important of all is that the reading teacher has to develop a feel for the 'occurrence of learning' (Prabhu 1987). This is because learning happens in a 'zone of proximal development' (Vygotsky 1978) or an 'i+1' zone (Krashen 1985). Adams (1990: 35) tells us that Jeanne Chall, the celebrated author of *Learning to Read: The Great Debate* (between phonics and whole word or whole language instruction), visited more than 300 kindergarten, 1st, 2nd and 3rd grade classrooms in the US, England and Scotland, located in wealthy, middle-class and poor districts. She found that differences in children's responsiveness to reading instruction were independent of the method, materials or objectives, and of class size and organisation. 'More than anything else, student engagement depended on the atmosphere—the momentum, support and expectations—created by the classroom teacher. ...the most weighty variable on this dimension was pace. It was the teacher's ability to stay tuned to that delicate interval between ease and difficulty for the students and to keep the instruction within it. ...interest and effort tended to wane when the children were left to unmonitored seatwork, especially with workbooks and worksheets.'

In the end, the teaching of reading relies above all on the knowledge, intuition and goodwill of the classroom teacher.

References

Adams, M. J., (1990). *Beginning to Read: Thinking and Learning about Print*. Cambridge, MA: MIT Press.

Amritavalli, R., (2007). *English in Deprived Circumstances: Maximizing Learner Autonomy*. Hyderabad: Foundation Books.

——— (2012). 'Helping children become readers'. *Language and Language Teaching*, 1/ 1, 1–4.

Goswami, U., (1999). 'Integrating orthographic and phonological knowledge as reading develops: Onsets, rimes and analogies in children's reading'. In Raymond Klein and Patricia McMullen (eds), *Converging Methods for Understanding Reading and Dyslexia*. Cambridge, MA: MIT Press.

Jangid, G. and R. Amritavalli, (2011). 'Whole language, story reading, and children's writing'. *The EFL Journal*, 2/ 2, 15–37.

Krashen, S. D., (1985). *The Input Hypothesis: Issues and Implications*. London: Longman.

Mangubhai, F., (2011). 'Reading, whole language, and second language learning: A personal journey'. *The EFL Journal*, 2/ 2, 1–13.

Nag, S. and M. Snowling, (2011). 'Reading comprehension, decoding skills and oral language'. *The EFL Journal*, 2/ 2, 85–105.

Prabhu, N. S., (1987). *Second Language Pedagogy*. Oxford: Oxford University Press.

Vygotsky, L. S., (1978). *Mind in Society: The Development of Higher Psychological Processes*. Cambridge, MA: Harvard University Press.

CHAPTER 7

'Speaking of food: Apple... ice-cream...posto...pesta... roti...'

RIMLI BHATTACHARYA

Abstract

Food as a theme is made visible and invisible in a number of ways in the school textbook. It straddles subjects as diverse as language-literature, geography, history, mathematics and science. However, 'food themes' and their vital links to the range of human experience and affects remain largely untapped, whether in conceptualising the pedagogy of textbooks or in actual classroom transactions. This paper sketches the continuum between the subjective and the historical contexts of food, with select examples from three language-literature textbooks in Bangla, Hindi and English. Through these examples I seek to address the following questions: How might we create links between individual experience and multiple histories of learners to enrich classroom activities? What kind of approaches would help teachers generate texts, exercises and projects? In what ways would an inter-disciplinary approach enable the learner to express herself and discover ways of establishing a relationship with our rapidly changing environment?

Introduction

In the early decades of the 21st century, children of the 'developing world' are exposed to a bewildering array of 'messages' through an unprecedented exposure to mass media. We live in a world where the 'click of a button' is meant to ensure global access. The harsh reality—particularly for first generation learners—is that the space of the classroom is continuously shrinking. A relentless dumbing down of the educational process is mistakenly/ mischievously identified as being democratic. A truly democratic classroom practice would encourage expression in many tongues, at least to begin with; provoke curiosity and questions; nurture the imagination *and* hone critical understanding. These are essential skills that the school has to provide to empower children, both *to mark changes* in their immediate worlds and eventually *to locate these changes* as larger processes, which we may provisionally call, history. What I call 'the food text' seems to have the potential for meeting many of these aspirations. But first, a few clarifications, to enable us to move beyond tokenism.

Beyond Tokenism

Very often, with the best of intentions, policy makers and textbook makers believe that a token inclusion of a minority/ marginal group's food is the way towards offering a 'multicultural' palette. Certainly, any substantive information (and knowledge) outside normative or mainstream practices is a welcome addition to any textbook. Unfortunately however, the foursome of food, festival, clothing and dance are often used exclusively as the *sole* markers of identity (as difference). Like in present day 'Food Courts' in shopping malls, there are many choices, but little by way of *distinctiveness* that can inform or shape the consumer's sensibilities in what is offered as 'ethnic' or 'exotic'.

For the State, or any institution and for many individuals who function as policy makers or educators, the festival seems to offer a readymade narrative: customs + food = togetherness = culture. Without adequate contextualisation, this approach has its pitfalls, as may be seen from a quick consideration of some NCERT textbooks, as for example, *Learning English* 3 (NCERT, 2002). In the later *Marigold* books (NCERT, 2008), Textbook V is the only one that deals in any detail with the issue of diverse cultures. It does so by including three folktales: 'Bamboo Curry'—a Santhal folktale;

'Avial'—a folktale from Kerala; and 'Who will be Ningthou?'—a Manipuri folktale. It is commendable that some thought has gone into the regional representation of language and place, and of communities who do not usually find representation in 'national' or pan-Indian textbooks: Santhali: Central/ Eastern India, Malayali: Southern India, and Manipuri: North-Eastern India.

And yet...there tends to be an implicit assumption in linking tribal and/or marginal cultures exclusively with folktales, as if the subjects do not have a life in experiential reality. Both the genre (in this case, the folktale) and the mode of representation (including the illustrations) fixes *them* in some timeless or fictional zone, different from *us* who are located in the contemporary world, alive and reading the text. In contrast, the very title of Mahasweta Devi's 'Kyun-kyun choRi', (chosen for the *Udaan* series, SCERT, 2004), with its emphasis on 'Why' challenges such a notion of an essentialised and unchanging identity. Clearly, unless the entire conceptual template is questioned or changed, 'the marginal' will only be 'included' *without* changing the actual terms of reference. This was evident in classroom observations of the transactions of texts such as 'Who will be Ningthou?' in *Marigold Textbook V* (Unit 9: 176), in Class VA of a Kendriya Vidyalaya in Delhi. (Bhattacharya & Madan 2012: 80–81).

If we wish to move beyond tokenism, or argue that difference is not to be found in a hierarchy, we may keep in mind the following considerations:

1. Whether in selecting/ creating the text, or in the exercises and activities that follow the text, the attempt should be to *contextualise socio-cultural practices* as a whole, rather than isolate and highlight only one feature. For, even a minority group will have many other features in common with the more mainstream groups. Rapid urbanisation and the proliferation of mass media have led to a shared vocabulary.
2. Linking the known to the unfamiliar is *to move beyond mere information* about the unfamiliar (e.g. some communities eat ants' eggs, or snakes and so on). An effective way of doing this is by privileging in the text and exercises, the subjectivity,

the emotional world of the person or people who is shown as doing something that might be unfamiliar to a large number of learners across the subcontinent.

3. The cycle of formal pedagogy requires that there should be a consolidation of the basics of language learning at every stage. Given their possible diversity, food texts are a powerful way of working with vocabulary, sounds in tandem with visual recognition of letters and words, and of *creating* narratives. The learner is thereby empowered to push the frontiers of the normative.
4. As the Editorial Invitation to his anthology highlighted, a first generation entrant to formal education is not a blank slate, but carries a world of linguistic and other resources that she brings to school. It is equally valid to examine if there are implicit or explicit prejudices already *normativised* in the language skills and cultural practices that children bring to school. If we agree with this second proposition, questions of tolerance and engagement beyond one's known or accepted beliefs can be aired through a critical exploration of any particular food theme.

The Subjective–Historical Continuum

How does food enter the classroom? The child may bring a snack to school, or buy one from vendors or the canteen; she may pick, find, forage and even filch something on the way.[1] More recently, the mandatory mid-day programme meal has effectively brought into a public arena what constitutes edible, nutritious, tasty food for a vast majority of children who are first generation learners. There is enough by way of official reports, informal observation and other sources for us to know that this compulsory mass feeding of children

[1] Embodied most movingly in Durga, the girl who is not sent to school and is at home in nature, in Bibhutibhushan Bandyopadhyay's *Pather Panchali* (1992), abridged for children as *Aam aanthir bhenpu* (translated as *Making a Mango Whistle*).

has myriad ramifications, detailing which are beyond the scope of this paper.[2] I shall suggest here that the very distinctions that are bound to crop up with regard to dietary habits, taste, taboos and so on in a communal space, may—if approached thoughtfully—be transformed into spaces for language learning and for opening up socio-cultural boundaries.

Let me elaborate on what I mean by the subjective-historical continuum. At the most basic level, any food item—raw or cooked!—has a history of production, transportation and consumption and pricing, which in turn includes the environment, geography, biological processes in relation to the weather, technology, human labour, and the shifting equilibrium in all of the above. Whatever we define as 'food' is thus inseparable from narratives of labour, occupation and cultural markers that may spill into questions of religion, ethnicity, caste and class and gender.[3]

Besides, there are certain normative assumptions of what may or may *not* find a place in the textbook. The question of appropriateness is usually vetted on what policy makers perceive is unfamiliar to a vast number of children (e.g. a fruit such as rambuttan), or offensive (as in the case of beef and ancient Indians), and ideally, should be open to debate.[4]

By the subjective, I mean the individual desires, fears, hopes and prejudices that the learner has already acquired and that she builds on in the course of formal education. Her relationship to the world of food is created through *a range of sensory experiences*, as much as it is by the presence and behaviour of people in her immediate environment. The subjective is therefore somewhat contingent on the kind of socialising she is exposed to. The learner as subject is also informed/ formed by more abstract historical forces which may include acts of legislation (for example, making the mid-day meal mandatory in schools) as well as latest techniques of branding in packaging food (for example,

[2] 'Report on the Mid-Day Meal', *The Pratichi Education Report II*, 132–35.

[3] For problematising children as workers/ labourers see an article by G. Alex in D. K. Behara (ed.) *Childhoods in South Asia.* 119–39.

[4] R. S. Sharma, *Communalism and History Textbooks.* 23.

a multinational company advocating a particular drink as 'health food' or 'truly Indian'.)

Fortunately though, history is present in more invisible ways as well. In the words of the eminent scholar D. D. Kosambi, 'history lies at our doorstep', such as the grinding stone still in use in most kitchens of the subcontinent.[5] The French historians were amongst the first to write a history of everyday life, which would include objects as well as practices. All three food-texts in this paper privilege the everyday.

My examples are drawn from SCERT and NCERT English (*Marigold*) and Hindi (*Udaan*) textbooks, and Bangla *Kishalay* Reader. This paper is part of a larger study; for reasons of space I have only offered a few examples from an entire range of textbooks and alternative publications that constitute the scope of my research. The examples here are not intended to be representative of any textbook series as a whole.

Mostafa Lives by the River Tista

Let us begin with the Bangla text, Lesson 2 of *Kishalay* 2, brought out by the West Bengal State Primary Board of Education.[6] (See Figure 7.1: *Kishalay* 2) In the example that follows, the narrative is presumably written by the textbooks makers, and not excerpted from any well-known 'author's' work, as is the case with almost all the poems in the same textbook. It is the second lesson of the literature textbook for class 2. The *Kishalay* series (first published in 1982; this being the 1999 reprint, and since replaced) was based on the competency-based approach, as has been emphasised in the 1996 preface included in the reprint. The chief competency that the student is expected to master is to recognise, read and write conjunct letters. My analysis of the text does not dwell on the merits

[5] As often emphasised by D. D. Kosambi in conversations with Kumar Shahani during the 1960s in Pune. Personal communication by Kumar Shahani.

[6] *Kishalay, Sahitya, dwitiya bhag.* (Bengali primer for Class II)(1982), Calcutta: 1999. Lesson 2, pp. 5–6.

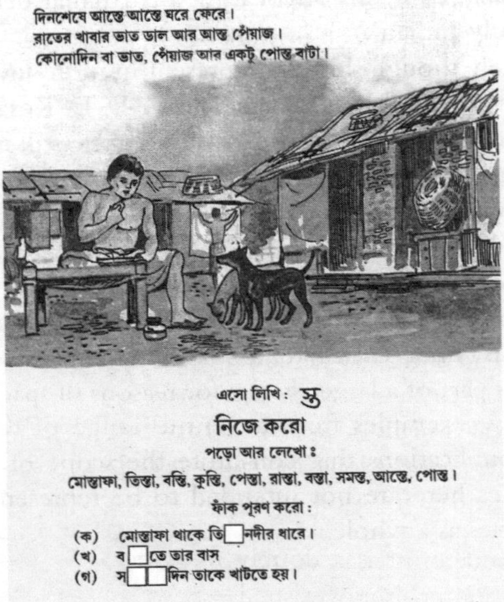

FIGURE 7.1 Mostafa

or demerits of 'competency-based learning'. Let us assume that the textbook writers and the teacher are obliged to work within the constraints of teaching conjunct letters (*sanjukto barno*): *s* + *t* = *st*.

The text has no title. I might call it 'Mostafa by the Tista'; and its subtext might well be 'the heroic in the everyday'. A rough translation follows:

mostafa thaake tistaa nodiir dhaare
'Mostafa lives on the banks of the Tista river.'
bostite taar aastana
'His home is in the *basti* (slum).'
roj bhore se kusti kare
'Early every morning, he wrestles/ goes wrestling.'
taarpare khae cholaa aar gur
'Then, he has a meal of gram and jaggery.'
baadaam pestaa paabe kothae.
'Where will he get almonds or pistachios!'

erpar hantadanta hoe kaaje jaaye
'After this, he rushes off to work.'
raastae lorry aase. bastaa-bastaa
'Lorries come to the roadside. He has to carry sacks and sacks'
maal boite hae gudaame
'full of load to the godown.'
samasta din taar khaatuni
'All day long he labours.'
The text continues on the following page:
dinSeSe aaste aaste ghare phere
'At the end of the day he slowly comes back home'
raater khaabaar bhaat daal aar aasto peaanj
'The meal at night is rice, dal and a whole onion.'
konodin baa bhaat, peaanj aar ektu posto baataa
'On some days it is rice, onion and some ground poppy seeds.'

The protagonist is a doubly marginalised figure: Mostafa is a Muslim labourer, impoverished—as we gather from the details of his diet, his living in a slum and so on. But he is exemplary if not 'heroic': he practices wrestling, he works hard all day, no negative qualities are ascribed to him, and he enjoys his simple fare. This appears to be the fairly straightforward message of the text, produced under the Left Front government in West Bengal.

What possibilities does the text offer beyond this exemplary figure? Interestingly, the very constraint of having to foreground conjunct letters fills the text with a range of rhythmic, sound-specific words that can generate new combinations. Reduplication abounds. There is assonance in the words *pesta* (pistacchio or almond) and *posto* (poppy seed); or *aasto* (whole) and *aaste-aaste* (slowly).

Neither of the two exercises that follow the text makes any effort to tap this link between sound and visual recognition of the conjunct. The first exercise asks the child to read out and write down all the words from the text with the *st* conjunct.[7] The second exercise has three fill-in–the-blanks, completely fact based.

[7] In Ishwarchandra Vidyasagar's hegemonic Bangla primer, *Barnaparichay*, Part II, conjunct letters are introduced with different vowel markers in the usual sequence; the learner is expected to work through the combinations like a drill.

The writer(s) may be commended for producing a fairly coherent narrative with the primary objective of introducing the child to a series of *st* conjunct words. However, in the exercises, the range of food words becomes *entirely incidental* to the learning experience. Ideologically, the narrative is intended to highlight the labour of the working man who is a Muslim, as suggested by the name. Let us assume that many of the learners are from poorer sections, or from minority communities, and have an experiential grasp of the situation suggested in the narrative or the three scenes. Does the teaching-learning experience address *their* likes and dislikes in any way? Is Mostafa's life meant to be information that has purely *one* pedagogical function: to fill in the blanks, to recognise/ read/ write conjunct letters?

There is enough in the text to work with the taste, texture or availability/context of food. For example making a table of whole object(s) *transformed* through grinding into a paste: *posto* (poppy seeds): *posto baata*; *peaanj* (onion): *peaanj baata*; *jiire* (cumin): *jiire baata*.

Sound drills, mapping the sound to the visual, could be created by categorising the conjunct letter in relation to the vowel sound: Tistaa and *pista*; *bosta* and *shosta*. Children are happy to make up nonsense words; they would internalise conjuncts better through creating their own words.

Some of the pleasure of reading is enunciated in the reduplicated sounds: *hanta-danta* or rushing/ huffing and puffing; *aaste-aaste* or slowly; *bosta-bosta* or sack loads. Lessons could be made with pairs of synonyms—*hanta-danta*: *tara-huro*; antonyms—*aaste-aaste*: *jode-jode* (slowly, fast/ hurriedly). Learners could discover other reduplications that suggest quantity: or sackfuls (to suggest many/ innumerable). Similarly, they could create a list of verbs with rhyme with *raasta* (road): e.g. *khaasta* (crisp). And why not toss in a riddle or two: What kind of fruit can you eat whole (*aasto)* and what do you need to peel or cut or chop?

Reduplication can have various semantic functions. For example, *bosta-bosta* suggests many or numerous. Other sentences: *Chhelera bari-bari giye chanda tole.* (The boys go from house to house collecting subscriptions.); or '*Grame-grame khobor chodiye gelo.*' (the news spread from one village to another).[8]

Why not encourage sentence-making both with and without the conjunct letters? Mostafa has to carry sack-loads of goods, unloading them from the truck and storing them in the godown: *bostaa-bostaa maal boite hae gudaame*. The verb '*boite hae*' can be used to speak about having to carry bags full of books …

The relationship between food, environment, livelihood and individual can emerge through questions functioning as cues:

1. Where *do you think* is the river Tista? (Correct information can be tested in senior classes, so that the same question would be 'Where *is* the Tista river?)
2. Is there a river near your village or town? What does it look like? What might the river Tista look like?
3. Why do you think Mostapha lives on the bank of the river Tista? Does the river flood? Where do you think he might go in that case?
4. What do you think is inside the *bosta* (sacks) that Mostapha unloads from the lorry? Why is it stored in the godown?
5. If Mostapha came to your home for a visit what would you like to offer him?
6. Make a list of the food you have for your mid-day meal at school, beginning with what you like most.

Children may be encouraged to draw/ paint their responses to any of the food items in the text, or make a story around them. The hungry dogs in the illustration add a subtle touch…there are leftovers even from those who have little to eat. Is it the hungry who can truly share?

With a Flick of the Wrist

Written in a sparkling conversational style, Pushpesh Pant's 'Roti' has found a place in *Udaan*, class 5, brought out by SCERT,

[8] Exercises 1 and 2 in the unit 'Shabdo ki baat': (Something about words), alerts the student to this range of usage, *Udaan* Class III, p. 41.

2004. This food text on Indian breads is a brilliant choice for several reasons, not the least because it has tremendous scope for tapping the multilinguality of the average classroom. 'Roti' covers a large part of the subcontinent, the focus being on north India, although the south finds a mention in the *appam*. Pant brings out the differences in the material, mode of making, contents, and accompaniments with each cereal—whether *roti*, *capaati*, *naan*, *kulcha*, *paranTha* or *shiirmal*.

The exercises are varied, ranging from the functional to the more imaginative. The first lot is information based, working with right or wrong, true or false. Some exercises encourage the learner to bring in her/ his individual home and environment into the frame of the classroom. Extremely generative is the question on vessels and equipment, emphasising size, shape, and material. This has the potential to bring in questions of science about heat, conductivity and metals: the various surfaces on which the roti is roasted, baked, toasted and the fuel used; the material and the mode; and the kind of temperatures needed for each and why. Students could be asked to illustrate any 'cooking scene' at home, on the footpath, in school….

More might be done with the texture, taste and the temperature of rotis that Pant's piece evokes. Can students be asked to recall any rhymes they know in their own language, which have to do with food? Why not compose their own rhymes or riddles? The name of the particular roti suggests something about its shape, how it is made and so on. Playing with words may encourage students to find out the histories of food: *rumaal: rumaali; capat: capaati*. There are several cues in the text which could be followed up: The capaati and 1857: How exactly was it used as a signal? What does it say about food habits of most of the soldiers? A sensitive topic on food proscriptions and taboos could be introduced: how they can make for bonding and inclusion or be turned into objects of instigation of hostility, riots and deaths. (e.g. The greased cartridge and the 1857 Revolt.)

There are rich cultural histories embedded in the text: How does food travel? In the course of changing environment and lifestyles, what would be the kinds of innovation and enrichment introduced? From their beginnings in nomadic cultures (e.g.

Central Asian cuisine) how do different kinds of rotis evolve meant for a more settled, courtly life? Does the *pao roti* have any link with *pao bhaji*? This would refer to the Portuguese and baked bread on the one hand, and street food introduced by migrants to Mumbai on the other, at very different points in history. Pizza is a kind of bread: How is it made in Italy? How did the recipe for pizza change when it travelled over the world? A larger connection may be made with leavened and unleavened; 'breaking bread' in every culture as a mark of friendship—bringing in the metaphorical resonances of food.

A possible class project would be to create a visual history of food around the theme of rotis from conception to consumption in

FIGURE 7.2 Making a ruumali roti

different venues (including the school). Imagine the raw material: grain of *baajra,* wheat/*genhu*, maize/*makai, jowaar*/sorghum—to—preparation—production—how consumed—season and climate… (Possible sources include the internet, encyclopaedia, to asking questions at home, speaking with people you know, or those in your neighbourhood who run restaurants and roadside vendors.)

If we agree that role of images in the textbook is not *merely* to illustrate (a for apple) but to convey something of the energy of the written text, the following sentence sums up the zesty language of this food-text: '*Banaane vale jyaadaa kalakaar ho to capaati ko apnii hathelii ke pichle bhaag me bithaakar hifaazat se khiincta-taantaa hava me uchaal kar rumaali roti ki shakl de deta hai.* (If the cook/maker is something of an artist then he will place the capaati on the back of his palm and skillfully pulling at it will toss it in the air and give it the shape of a rumaali roti.) The lackadaisical static representation does not match up. (See Figure 7.2)

But what is Food?

Udaan for class 5 also has Mahasweta Devi's classic '*Kyun-kyun choRi"* (Lesson 15, pp. 61–66). The story works with a sophisticated frame. The first person narrator—an educated urban adult, it is implied, turns out to be naïve in some ways in confronting the insatiable curiosity and dynamism of the ten-year old Moina, who is from the Shabor tribe. The narrative begins: A little chit of a girl she was, running after a big snake. (*chotii si laRkii thii voh…. ek baRe se saanp ka piichaa kar rahii thii.*) When the adult forbids the child to do so, she is informed: 'You know we eat snakes. Chop off the head, sell the skin and cook the meat and eat it up.' (*pata hai ham saanp khaate hain. mundi kaat do, camraa bec do, maas pakaakar kha lo.*) Later, there is a reference to how wonderfully her mother Khiri cooks snake meat: 'The good/edible snakes I catch and give them [to my mother]. Such wonderful snake meat she cooks in toddy.' *(achii vale saanpo ko mai pakaR kar bhi de deti hun. Kyaa baRhiaa tariivaalaa saanp banaati hai maa.)* (p. 63) Through such marvelously crisp sentences we are alerted to a different economy of survival.[9] Of knowledge being of different kinds. Of a young girl teaching an adult about another kind of life. Moina's everyday may seem unfamiliar/strange to many, but *it is part of her subjectivity*, her history, her life.[10]

Many stories and autobiographies written by Dalit writers have repeatedly focused on the pain, humiliation and also the reality of having to eat only leftovers, of their touch being treated as polluting food and water (*Jhootan*).[11] As texts, these would be considered too grim, brutal, at the primary and early secondary school level. Pointing to the glaring inequities of our system they might be considered politically 'sensitive'. Yet another complication to any simplistic politics of 'inclusion.' Further, there is an increasing exorcising in the public domain of eating habits and customs that might initiate protests and eventually censorship because of 'hurt sentiments.' The deletion of sections from NCERT textbooks in 2000 is a case in point. (Sahmat 2002).

Censorship, whether self-imposed or dictated from above, is not confined to the discipline of history. It is so pervasive that the three selections presented above are to be commended for the potential they hold. In speaking of food, one asks: Is the textbook permitted to raise (even if indirectly) uncomfortable questions? Would an exposure to the 'unfamiliar' or the 'suppressed' actually enable an understanding beyond the immediate connection made in the text? Is the role of language to enable us to know something about the other?

CONCLUSION

Our answers to these questions just posed would certainly be in the affirmative. But, there might be legitimate anxieties about

[9] The illustrations to this lesson go against the grain of the text in every way. See Fig. 4, Udaan, Class V, p. 61.

[10] For a brilliant exploration of space, colour and subjectivity and an interplay between adult and adolescent perspectives, see artist Gulammohammed Sheikh's rendering of Mohammed Khadeer Babu's Telegu story translated as *Head Curry*, Anveshi, 2008.

[11] See for example, the title story in *Poisoned Bread*, Arjun Dangle (ed.) Hyderabad: Orient BlackSwan, 2009, pp. 167–176.

the 'uncomfortable' not being immediately identified and then denounced as 'offensive'. An anxiety that, by encouraging, even inviting 'difference' into the classroom, is there an alienation of those who hold mainstream or normative positions. However, the classroom is precisely the space where one may learn fearlessly and thoughtfully.

We might wish to further explore/ extend the potential of the diverse texts we have considered in this essay, in terms of the following benchmarks:

1. Does the narrative (prose or poem), whether as reported speech or as a first person narrative, offer the learner a sympathetic entry into a world that is perceived as outside of a comfortable middle-class existence? (It could be a world within our world whether it is of the urban poor, or the rural agricultural worker?
2. Does it allow one whether as teacher or learner to link the detail of the everyday material world with larger processes brought about by changes in the world, in the country or in the region? For example, what might be the links between the particular ingredient or raw material, a larger trend, abstract questions of nutrition, economy, land and labour, and so on?
3. Do the 'exercises' around food conjure up something of the sheer pleasure that we all associate with food, its appeal to the senses, its synaesthetic possibilities?

Here the challenge would be to counter the hegemonic language of advertisements by multinationals in all kinds of media, particularly television, where food/drinks are imaged with hugely sophisticated technological means, backed by huge funds!

References

Alex, Gabriele, (2007). 'Work versus education: Children's everyday life in rural Tamil Nadu'. In Deepak Kumar Behara (ed.), *Childhoods in South Asia*. New Delhi: Pearson Longman, 119–39.

Babu, Mohammed Khadeer, (2008). 'Head Curry'. Translated from Telegu by A. Suneetha. Illustrated by Gulammohammed Sheikh. *Different Tales*. Anveshi and Parag. Kerala: D.C. Books.

Bandyopadhyay, Bibhutibhushan, (2007). *Making a Mango Whistle* (*Aam Anthir Bhepu*). Translated from Bengali to English by Rimli Bhattacharya. New Delhi: Puffin Classic Series.

Bhattacharya, Rimli & Anuja Madan (eds), (2012). *Notes on Running Feet. English in Primary Textbooks*. Bhopal: Eklavya.

Dangle, Arjun (ed.), (2009). *Posioned Bread*. Hyderabad: Orient BlackSwan.

Devi, Mahasweta, (2004). 'Kyun-kyun choRi'. In *Udaan*, Hindi Textbook, Class V. Delhi: SCERT, Lesson 15, 61–66.

Menon, Usha, (2003). 'Where Have the mangoes gone?' *Economic and Political Weekly*, 38/18 (May 3–9), 1747–49.

Pratichi, (2009). *The Pratichi Education Report II. Primary Education in West Bengal, changes and challenges.* Delhi: Pratichi (India) Trust, 132–35.

Kishalay, Sahitya, dvitya bhag. (Bengali primer for Class II) (1982), Calcutta: rpt. 1999. Lesson 2 (untitled), 5–6.

Pant, Pushpesh, (2004). 'Roti'. In *Udaan*, Hindi Textbook, Class V. Delhi: SCERT, Lesson 7, 26–30.

Communalisation of Education. The Assault on History. Press Reportage, Editorials and Articles. (2002) New Delhi: Sahmat.

CHAPTER 8

General Semantics, Neuro-Linguistic Programming and Language in the Classroom[1]

PRAMOD PANDEY AND ARUNA KORNANA

Abstract

The central tenet of Neuro-Linguistic Programming (NLP) may be said to lie in the statement 'The Map is not the Territory'. That is, we operate in this world on the basis of the map of the world and not the world itself. An awareness of the blocks, limitations, and distortions of the map can help us grow out of them and come closer to reality. The origin of the tenet goes back to General Semantics, founded by Alfred Korzybsky with the aim of developing scientific awareness about bringing language closer to reality, in order to avoid misevaluations and conflicts in the world of human interaction and to free ourselves from individual proclivities and biases. In this paper, we attempt to show how a concern with an understanding of the learner's map of the world, the teacher can help her overcome her limitations and offer her greater choices of growth. We begin with a discussion of the evidence for universal and cultural cognitive dispositions to language, drawing from the linguistic and pragmatic literature. We then briefly bring up for elaboration some of the basic concepts of NLP. We finally discuss the results of an NLP based experiment on a group of BEd students specialising in English in support of the claim.

[1] We are grateful to Dr Balachandra Vishnu Adkoli, KL Wig Centre for Medical Education & Technology, AIIMS, New Delhi, for giving us time for a very useful discussion on administering the questionnaires and their analyses.

Introduction

Epistemologists and educationists have held two main aspects of the human mind/ brain of central concern. These are language and reasoning. Philosophers (for example, positivists, such as Ayer (1936) and ordinary language philosophers, such as Ryle (1949) and scientists (in fields as diverse as physics, economics, evolutionary biology and ecology) have found ordinary language a hindrance in expressing abstract ideas (see e.g. Mermin 2005) and have looked for a language that facilitates rather than hinders expression of thought. Reasoning is concerned with being valid and sound in ascertaining knowledge. Alfred Korzybsky (1940) founded an area of inquiry known as General Semantics, which is centrally concerned with both. In his view, the '...human world in which we live is based on science... and therefore on non-Euclidian, non-Newtonian and non-Aristotelian systems, yet our inherited orientations remain Aristotelian, Euclidian, and Newtonian...'. General semantics aims to show the way how valid and sound reasoning can develop in ways that are congenial to science, and how scientific awareness about language can make it come closer to reality in order to avoid misevaluations and conflicts in the world of human interaction. Germane to general semantics is the goal of attaining freedom from biases and miscommunication. General Semantics set the epistemological groundwork for Neuro-Linguistic Programming (NLP), a theory of communication (see Bandler & Grinder 1979; Andreas & Faulkner 1996; Dilts & DeLozier 2000; Knight 2002; Tosey & Mathison 2006), which shares Korzybsky's basic idea that human beings are limited in what they know by the structure of both their nervous systems, and the structure of human languages. As a result, human beings cannot experience the world directly, but only through what he called their 'abstractions'.

Learning is a process that involves transformation. A teacher faces the challenge of bringing in transformation in students leading them from a given state to a desired state. The distance between these states is different for different individuals and the path between them has to be chosen by the teacher considering the different channels of perception of each individual. Some individuals develop anxieties, aversions, beliefs, passions and preferences at an early stage. Some patterns and beliefs help while others limit us in achieving what we want.

In a language classroom, it is crucial for the teacher to understand students' beliefs about learning a second or a foreign language (see e.g. Horwitz 1988; Rifkin 2000), as the beliefs may impact positively or detrimentally in learning a language. Learning English as a second language involves internalising the grammar and its components (phonetics, phonology, morphology, syntax and semantics) as well structures of contextual meaning and use, by mainly paying attention to what is presented in the classroom. In addition, there are issues related to the learner's psychological disposition such as confidence, self-esteem and spontaneity that affect the learning. A language teacher has to create an environment where students are disposed to learn not only *what* but also *how*. Teachers can motivate learners and help them shed their anxieties by making them aware of their inherent capabilities. New approaches have been identified to enable the teacher to induce this kind of learning. NLP is one such approach.

This paper aims at understanding the role of NLP in the classroom and providing evidence for the claim that the NLP techniques impact the learner's as well as the teacher's thinking and language patterns. We begin first with a brief discussion of evidence for universal and cultural cognitive dispositions to language, drawing from the linguistic and pragmatic literature in support of the NLP position that we are linguistically and culturally predisposed to a subjective view of reality. We then bring up for elaboration some of the basic concepts of NLP with regard to the ways in which we can inculcate positive dispositions to teaching and learning. We finally discuss the results of an NLP-based experiment on a group of B.Ed. students undergoing preschool teacher training at the English and Foreign Languages University, in support of the claim. Given the limited time for the experiment, it was aimed at showing the impact on thinking and representational pattern of the learner.

Uncertainty of Sensory Experience and Language

The assumption common to General Semantics and NLP that 'the map is not the territory', i.e., there exists a mismatch between the world of reality and our interpretation of it, is strongly supported by the evidence that has gained ground for both variability and unreliability of sensory perceptions and language as a source of objective knowledge since the time of Descartes. We briefly discuss here the evidence for the predispositions for subjectivity of understanding and interpretation.

We first turn to the differences in sensory perceptions. Mohanan (2011) gives the following example: 'Bill and Susan are in the same room. Bill finds the room warm, while Susan finds it cold. The objective reality of the *temperature* of the room is the same, but their sensory experience of *warm/cold* is different for the two individuals. Such differences in the subjective experience of *warm/cold* are quite natural if Susan has high fever and Bill doesn't.'

Just as sensory experiences are different, meaning in language too, is different at all levels—word, sentence and utterance. At the word level, consider a familiar example, *book*, used in different senses:

(1) a. The book weighs a kilo.
b. The book is full.
c. I have the book in my pen drive.
d. She knows the book by heart.
e. The writer has yet to complete the book.

and so on.

In (1) above, the word *book* is used in different senses in each of the sentences. Abstract terms such as *bright*, *democracy* and *freedom* have been known in positivist philosophy to be subject to variable interpretation. Modern linguistic literature is full of examples of phrasal (e.g. *Egyptian cotton shirt*, understood as either 'a shirt made of Egyptian cotton' or 'a cotton shirt manufactured in Egypt'), syntactic (e.g. *Visiting relatives can be dangerous*, understood differently on basis of the word *visiting* being considered a verb or an adjective) and pragmatic (e.g. *It is raining* may have the implication 'Get me an umbrella' or 'I can't go out now' or some other message). We avoid dwelling on the topic here because of its familiarity in the literature.

More interesting and somewhat in line with Linguistic Relativity or Sapir–Whorf Hypothesis (see. Kay & Kempton 1984; Gumperz & Levinson 1996) are cases of linguistic categories influencing a speaker's understanding of the world. Many studies in favour (e.g. Brown & Lenneberg 1954; Olson 1977; Boroditsky, Schmidt & Phillips 2003) and against linguistic relativity (e.g. Pinker 1995, 1997) have been presented in recent times. A case in point here is conceptual gender in languages that categorise objects in different gender categories. Boroditsky, Schmidt & Phillips (2003: 69) discuss how grammatical gender in a language may influence not only the speaker's understanding of the concept they stand for but also other decisions. They explain the role of conceptual gender thus:

> What does it mean for a turnip to be conceptually feminine or for a toaster to be conceptually masculine? How does gender actually make its way into the representations of objects? As suggested earlier, one possibility is that, depending on grammatical gender, different (stereotypically masculine or feminine) aspects of objects may become more or less salient in the representations of those objects. For example, if the noun that names a toaster is masculine, then perhaps its metallic and technological properties may become more salient; but if the noun is feminine, then perhaps its warmth, domesticity, and ability to provide nourishment are given more importance.

Boroditsky et al. (2003) report the results of an experiment on Spanish and German speaking children for the use of adjectives for objects that are categorised differently for grammatical gender in their languages. For example, the word 'bridge' is feminine in German and masculine in Spanish. The children were asked to tick the adjectives that suited the words from a list of the adjectives given to them along with the words. They report (p. 69), '…the word "key" is masculine in German and feminine in Spanish. German speakers described keys *as hard*, *heavy*, *jagged*, *metal*, *serrated*, and *useful*, while Spanish speakers said they were *golden*, *intricate*, *little*, *lovely*, *shiny*, and *tiny*. The word for "bridge", on the other hand, is feminine in German and masculine in Spanish. German speakers described bridges as *beautiful*, *elegant*, *fragile*, *peaceful*, *pretty*, and *slender*, while Spanish speakers said they were *big*, *dangerous*, *long*, *strong*, *sturdy* and *towering*.'

Neuro-Linguistic Programming

NLP was developed in the 1970's jointly by Richard Bandler, a mathematician and a graduate student of psychology, and John Grinder, a linguist, originating in their attempt to model excellent communication by investigating the communicative behaviour of reputed communicators in the field of psychotherapy. The latter included names such as Fritz Perls, the innovative psychotherapist and originator of the Gestalt school of therapy, Virginia Satir, one of the key figures in the development of family therapy, and Milton Erickson, a psychiatrist who specialised in medical hypnosis. Bandler & Grinder initially explored in these excellent communicators their patterns of language and behaviour, their thinking processes and their core beliefs. All three of them had different personalities but Bandler & Grinder found that they all followed similar patterns in relating to their clients, in the language they used, and in the beliefs they held about themselves and what they were doing (Revell & Norman 1999). Bandler & Grinder's aim was to produce a model of successful therapy that worked in practice, and could be learned. The underlying assumption of their research was that all human beings have the same neurology and, therefore, the behaviour of effective communicators can be modelled, learned and taught.

They emphasised the fact that we communicate about our experiences to ourselves and to others through two means, Neuro and Linguistic. The two could be combined into a single approach to the study of effective communication called Neuro-Linguistic Programming. 'The "Neuro" part of NLP acknowledges the fundamental idea that all behaviour stems from our neurological processes of sight, hearing, smell, taste, touch, and feeling. We experience the world through our five senses; we make "sense" of the information and then act on it. Our neurology covers not only our invisible thought processes, but also our visible physiological reactions to ideas and events. One simply reflects the other at the physical level. Body and mind form an inseparable unity, a human being.' (O'Connor & Seymour 1990: 3). 'The "Linguistic" part of the title indicates the way the language shapes, as well as reflects, our experience of the world. We use language—in thought as well as in speech—to represent the world to ourselves, and to embody our beliefs about the world and about life. If we change the way we speak and think about things, we can change our behaviour. We can also use language to help other people who want to change.' (Revell & Norman, 1999: 14) The 'Programming' refers to ways we can choose to organise our ideas and actions to produce results.

NLP deals with showing how we structure our subjective experience—how we organise what we see, hear and feel, and how we edit and filter the outside world through our senses. Being aware of our subjective proclivities of reasoning and representation can lead to our rising above them as well as expanding them, and in turn helping others, in our case the learner, in achieving the same.

NLP was originally portrayed as a method, which the authors called 'modelling' (Bandler & Grinder 1975: 6). Stemming from Bandler & Grinder's original interest in identifying what distinguished excellent therapists from others, and informed by Grinder's knowledge of linguistics, NLP began as a means of studying how individuals process information, construct meaning schemas, and perform skills to achieve results. Bandler & Grinder, in their book *Frogs into Princes*, emphasised on pragmatic intent: 'We have no idea about the "real" nature of things, and we're not particularly interested in what's "true". The function of modelling is to arrive at descriptions which are useful.' (p. 7)

Assumptions and Techniques of NLP Analysis

NLP aims at helping individuals cross the barriers that have a basis in their mental dispositions and that can be uncovered by analysing their linguistic expressions and thought processes. NLP begins with getting to the roots of lack of motivation in learners by analysing the preferred representational systems, on the one hand (for example, some individuals prefer listening to reading or sounds to written symbols, and do better if given a task in the preferred mode of representation). It then works towards improving motivation for learning and developing self-reliance in the learner through its basic assumptions and techniques such as ANCHORING, REFRAMING, OUTCOME THINKING and RAPPORT BUILDING. These are explained briefly below.

Assumptions of NLP

Assumptions of NLP are about human behaviour, experience, communication and potential that influence an individual's thinking and behaviour. Achieving excellence is helped if we act as if these beliefs were true. Some of the main beliefs of excellence (Revell & Norman 1997) that guide the application of NLP in language learning are as follows.

a. If someone can do something, anyone can *learn* to do it.
b. The map is not the territory: what we perceive about the world and others around us is not the actual reality, as our senses filter most of what we experience. It is entirely our reality. So every learner experiences reality in their own way. We all have different maps of the world.
c. Each person is unique: as every individual has his own way of filtering the information while experiencing the world, they have unique ways of learning a language.
d. The meaning of communication is the response you get: communication is not one's intention, it is the experiential process.
e. There is no failure, only feedback: all experience is learning and a renewed opportunity for success, considering mistakes as sources of learning.
f. Mind and body are parts of the same system: thoughts, emotions and behaviour are interconnected.
g. We have within us all the resources we will ever need: whether it is confidence, self-esteem or spontaneity, we have them within us already. Although we may not have these resources in a certain context, we may have them in some other context.

h. Communication is non-verbal as well as verbal: as a teacher, one needs to be aware of their own language, gestures, attitudes, appearances, and the messages they are giving as for language learners it's not just the linguistic aspect that helps but also the non-verbal interaction.
i. Communication is non-conscious as well as conscious: according to Dr Emile Donchin at the University of Illinois, more than 99% of our learning is non-conscious. According to Revell & Norman, learning seems to be more effective when it is multi-sensory and when it appeals to the non-conscious as well as conscious mind.

Techniques of NLP

Some of the main techniques used in NLP training are aimed at awakening the creative potentials of individuals by developing an insight into their cognitive proclivities and then matching learning techniques to the realisation of their potentials. These are broached below.

a. 'Anchoring' involves making the learner hold to resourceful states when his confidence is low. The teacher needs to find out from the learner his/ her qualities of strength and turn to them in times of difficulties for the learner.
b. 'Reframing' helps change focus from negative or indifferent to positive expressions, as, for example, 'I have poor spoken English' can be reframed as 'I want to improve my spoken English', and 'I should write well' can be reframed as 'I want to write well'.
c. 'Outcome thinking' is the assumption that the way we think about our goals decides how efficiently and quickly we are going to achieve them. A learner who says, 'I am not going to keep quiet in class' is less likely to participate in learning than the one who says 'I am going to take an active part in the activities of the class'.
d. 'Rapport building' involves improving the relationship between communicators, in our case the teacher and the learner, through compatible matching of verbal and non-

verbal expressions. The focus is communication, and the methods involve making the learner self-aware of his/ her potential capabilities and help him/ her develop a strongly positive mental disposition to communication.

We have attempted above to broach some of the critical concepts of NLP. For more detailed discussion, the reader may look up O'Connor & Seymour (1990) and Knight (2002), among others.

Experimental Study

The role of NLP as an analytical tool in uncovering the reasoning patterns in an individual has been widely recognised by its practitioners (Lum 2001; Knight 2002; Pandey 2010). However, its role in affecting the thinking and language patterns of individuals has come to be seen as controversial, with opposite claims being made by its advocates (Revell & Norman 1997, 1999 for language teaching) and its detractors (Sharpley 1984; Roderique-Davies 2009). Roderique-Davies (2009), for example, claims that NLP 'does not have an evidence base and that NLP practitioners are seeking a post-hoc credibility.' In the field of language teaching, the situation is still exploratory (Revell & Norman 1997, 1999; Craft 2001; Gupta 2008). In order to ascertain the validity of the claims of NLP in the field of language teaching and learning, a preliminary study (Kornana 2012) was carried out, in consultation with the first author, on the possibility of change of preference patterns in the learner as part of his/ her thinking and reasoning patterns. The working hypothesis of the study was that the intervention of NLP will have an effect on the individual's preferences. Towards that end, it was felt necessary to devise reliable psychological tests for the preference patterns following and preceding an NLP workshop.

Preference patterns in Myers-Briggs Type Indicator

The preference patterns that were the focus of the workshop were the Myers-Briggs personality types, also known as Myers-Briggs Type Indicators (MBTI), widely followed for psychological test of personality types today (Quenk 2009). The classification of personality types involves four main sets of dichotomy, namely, Extraversion (E)–Introversion (I), Sensing (S)–Intuition (N), Thinking (T)–Feeling(F), and Judging (J)–Perceiving (P). Their main traits are as elaborated below.

a. **Sensing (S):** Focuses mainly on what can be perceived by the five senses.
   Intuition (N): Focuses mainly on perceiving patterns and interrelationships.
b. **Thinking (T):** Bases conclusions on logical analysis with a focus on objectivity and detachment.
   Feeling (F): Bases conclusions on personal or social values with a focus on understanding and harmony.
c. **Extraversion (E):** Directs energy mainly towards the outer world of people and objects.
   Introversion (I): Directs energy mainly towards the inner world of experiences and ideas.
d. **Judging (J):** Prefers the decisiveness and closure that results from dealing with the outer world using one of the judging processes (T or F).
   Perceiving (P): Prefers the flexibility and spontaneity that results from dealing with the outer world using one of the perceiving processes (T or F).

Each of the four dichotomies has its variant facets, as elaborated in Table 8.1.

TABLE 8.1 The four MBTI dichotomies and facets

Opposite functions of perception		*Opposite functions of judging*	
Sensing	**Intuition**	**Thinking**	**Feeling**
Concrete	Abstract	Logical	Empathetic
Realistic	Imagination	Reasonable	Compassionate
Practical	Conceptual	Questioning	Accommodating
Experiential	Theoretical	Critical	Accepting
Traditional	Original	Tough	Tender

(contd...)

(Table 8.1 contd...)

Opposite attitudes of energy		*Opposite attitude toward the outside world*	
Extraversion	**Introversion**	**Judging**	**Perceiving**
Initiating	Receiving	Systematic	Casual
Expressive	Contained	Planful	Open-ended
Gregarious	Intimate	Early starting	Pressure prompted
Active	Reflective	Scheduled	Spontaneous
Enthusiastic	Quiet	Methodical	Emergent

The four MBTI dichotomous sets have their communicational patterns, projected in Table-8.2.

TABLE 8.2 Communication facets of the MBTI dichotomies

The Sensing-Intuition Dichotomy	
Concrete Focuses on concrete, tangible, and literal perceptions, communications, learning styles, world view, and values. Trusts what is verifiable by the senses, and is cautious about going beyond facts.	*Abstract* Focuses on concepts and abstract meanings of ideas and their interrelationships. Uses symbols, metaphors, and mental leaps to explain interests and views.
The Thinking-Feeling Dichotomy	
Questioning Asks questions to understand, clarify, gain common ground, solves problems, and finds flaws in their own and others' viewpoints.	*Empathetic* Believes that the impact of a decision on people should be primary; focuses on important values and relationships; trusts own appraisal of what is relevant.
The Extraversion—Introversion Dichotomy	
Active Likes direct involvement in active environments, learning best by	*Reflective* Likes visual, intellectual, and mental engagement, learning best by

(contd...)

(Table 8.2 contd...)

doing, listening, observing, and speaking rather than by reading and writing.	reading and writing rather than by listening and speaking.
The Judging and Perceiving Dichotomy (likes and dislikes)	
Planful Likes the comfort and security of working with routine, established methods both at work and at home; like the predictability this gives their lives.	*Open-ended* Likes flexible plans and freedom to choose in the moment; dislike being tied down by long-range plans and prior commitments.

Table 8.2: Communication facets of the MBTI dichotomies (adapted from Quenk 2009: 10–12)

Based on MBTI, we had eight function-attitudes and sixteen personality types, listed below.

Introverted sensing: ISTJ and ISFJ
Extraverted sensing: ESTP and ESFP
Introverted intuition: INTJ and INFJ
Extraverted intuition: ENTP and ENFP
Introverted thinking: ISTP and INTP
Extraverted thinking: ESTJ and ENTJ
Introverted feeling: ISFP and INFP
Extraverted feeling: ESFJ and ENFJ

Subjects, questionnaires and their analyses

Two questionnaires were used—Questionnaire-1 and Questionnaire-2. Questionnaire-1 was administered at the start of the workshop, while Questionnaire-2 was administered at the end of the workshop. Both the questionnaires were based on Keirsey Temperament Sorter (KTS). The first questionnaire was taken from Keirsey & Bates (1984) and the second questionnaire was taken from the Keirsey website.[2] The purpose of using two versions of the KTS sorter was

[2] http: //www.keirsey.com/personalityzone/cz1.asp

to avoid predictable response. In the second questionnaire, some of the questions were reframed. Both the questionnaires were analysed using the Myers-Briggs Type Indicator [MBTI, as elaborated in Quenk (2009)]. Both questionnaires consisted of 70 questions; 10 questions belonging to Extraversion (E)–Introversion (I) dichotomy and 20 questions each for the other three dichotomies, namely, Sensing (S)–iNtuition (N), Thinking (T) –Feeling (F), and Judging (J)–Perceiving (P). It should be noted that both questionnaires were used as a tool to identify the preferences, and did not involve any scaling and value.

The workshop was conducted three days a week in slots of 1 to 2 hours for a period of 3 weeks in February and March 2012. The total duration of the workshop was 13 classroom hours. The subjects were final semester students undergoing teacher training for the BEd programme in English at the English and Foreign Languages University, Hyderabad.

A total of 29 participants filled Questionnaire-1 and 33 participants filled Questionnaire-2. Nineteen students filled both the questionnaires. All the questionnaires were interpreted for results. However, questionnaires of only 19 participants, who filled in both sets, were used for research purpose as the objective was to identify the difference in their preferences. While analysing the data, questionnaires of 3 more participants had to be left aside because they omitted more than 20 questions in one of the questionnaires and according to Myers-Briggs, three to four omissions on any dichotomy can produce a problematic scoring situation. Therefore, the responses of only 16 participants were used for data analysis. Of the 16 participants, 6 were female and 10 male. All were in the age group of 22–28 years, and came from different parts of India. All the responses were scored for raw points; once the data collection procedure was complete. A scoring template was used for scoring the responses, which gave the raw points for each preference pole of the dichotomies. The pole of each dichotomy that had the larger number of raw points was identified as the respondent's preference on that dichotomy.

However, if there were equal points on both the poles of a dichotomy they were classified as I, N, F, or P, depending on the dichotomy. The convention of breaking tied scores in this fashion was set by Isabel Briggs Myers when she constructed previous forms of the Indicator. The basic rationale is that ties are broken in favour of the preference pole that is less common or sanctioned in the population at large: A person with split votes on a dichotomy is indicating a pull toward the less popular pole, which may be counteracted by an equal pull toward the more popular pole. The likely preference is therefore hypothesised to be the less popular one. In this reasoning, for example, a person with equal points for E and I is going against the tide that favours an extraverted approach and is therefore probably truly an Introvert struggling to accommodate to what is socially desirable (Quenk 2009: 48).

An individual's preferences were then summarised in a four-letter code, each letter standing for one of the eight preferences, such as INFP for Introverted, Intuitive, Feeling, Perceiving or ESTJ for Extraverted, Sensing, Thinking, Judging. All possible combinations of preferences yield 16 different types.

All 16 types are seen as valid and legitimate ways of being psychologically healthy, adapted, and successful, though their interests, talents, and general outlooks are likely to be quite different (Quenk 2009: 9).

Questionnaire results: Questionnaire 1

This questionnaire, as was mentioned above, was administered at the beginning of the workshop. In the evaluation it showed that out of 16 participants, 9 participants had the preference type ESFJ (Extraverted Feeling) that constituting 56.25% of the total, 3 participants had the preference type ISTJ (Introverted Sensing) that constituted 18.75% of the total, and the other 4 participants showed the preference type ISFJ, INFJ, ISTP, and ESTJ, respectively, that constituted to 6.25% each of the total. Of the 16 types, 10 types constituted 0% of the total. These findings are displayed in the table below.

TABLE 8.3 The distribution of personality types among the participants before the NLP workshop

ISTJ 18.75% Introverted	ISFJ 6.25%	ESTP 0%	ESFP 0%	25% Sensing type
INTJ 0%	INFJ 6.25%	ENTP 0%	ENFP 0%	6.25% Intuitive type
ISTP 6.25%	INTP 0%	ESTJ 6.25%	ENTJ 0%	12.5% Thinking type
ISFP 0%	INFP 0%	ESFJ 56.25% Extraverted	ENFJ 0%	56.25% Feeling type
25%	12.5%	62.5%	00%	N=16

Questionnnaire results: Questionnaire-2

Questionnaire–2, as mentioned above, was administered at the end of the workshop. The evaluation showed that out of the 16 participants, 8 participants had the preference type ESFP (Extraverted Sensing) constituting 50% of the total, 2 participants had the preference type ISFP (Introverted Feeling) constituting 12.5% of the total, 2 participants preference type ISFJ (Introverted Sensing) constituting 12.5% of the total, and the other 4 participants showed preference types ISTJ, INFJ, ENTP, and ENTJ, respectively, constituting 6.25% each of the total. Of the 16 types, 9 types constituted 0% of the total. These findings are displayed overleaf in Table 8.4.

Discussion

The results of the responses to the questionnaires are present in the graphs (Figures 8.1, 8.2, and 8.3).

On a comparison of the responses to the two questionnaires and their analysis using MBTI criteria, we notice a considerable change in the preference types of the participants as a consequence of the

TABLE 8.4 The distribution of personality types among the participants after the NLP workshop

ISTJ 6.25%	ISFJ 12.5% Introverted	ESTP 0%	ESFP 50% Extraverted	68.75% Sensing type
INTJ 0%	INFJ 6.25%	ENTP 6.25%	ENFP 0%	12.5% Intuitive type
ISTP 0%	INTP 0%	ESTJ 0%	ENTJ 6.25%	6.25% Thinking type
ISFP 12.5% Introverted	INFP 0%	ESFJ 0%	ENFJ 0%	12.5% Feeling type
18.75%	18.75%	6.25%	56.25%	N=16

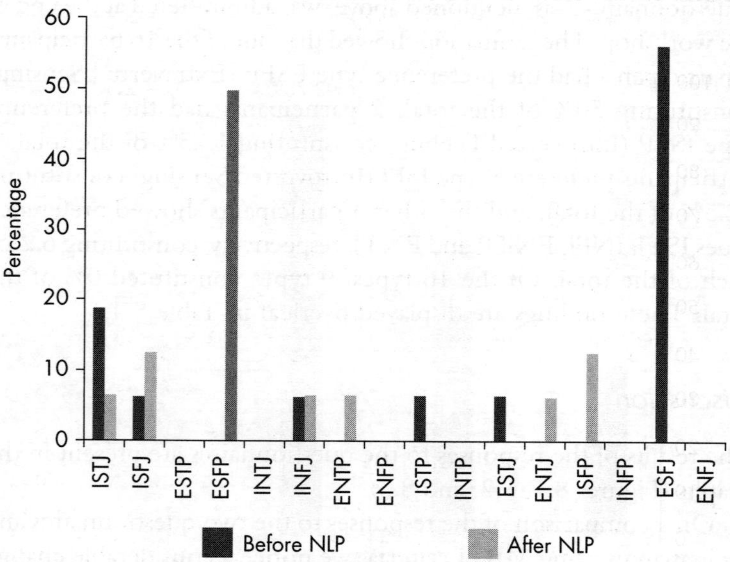

FIGURE 8.1 Results based on Personality type (in percentage)

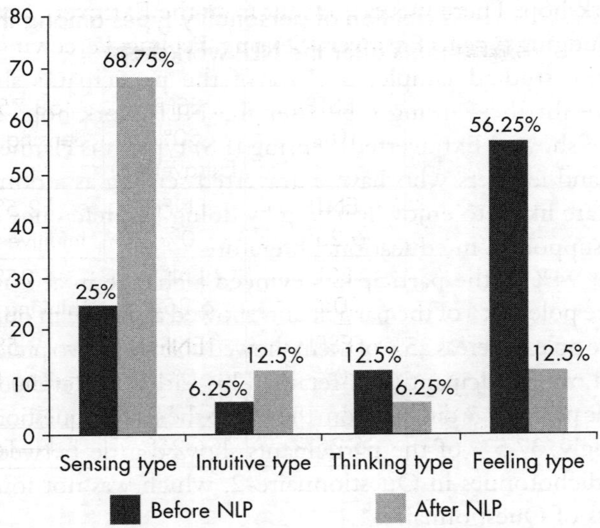

FIGURE 8.2 Results based on attitude preferences (in percentage)

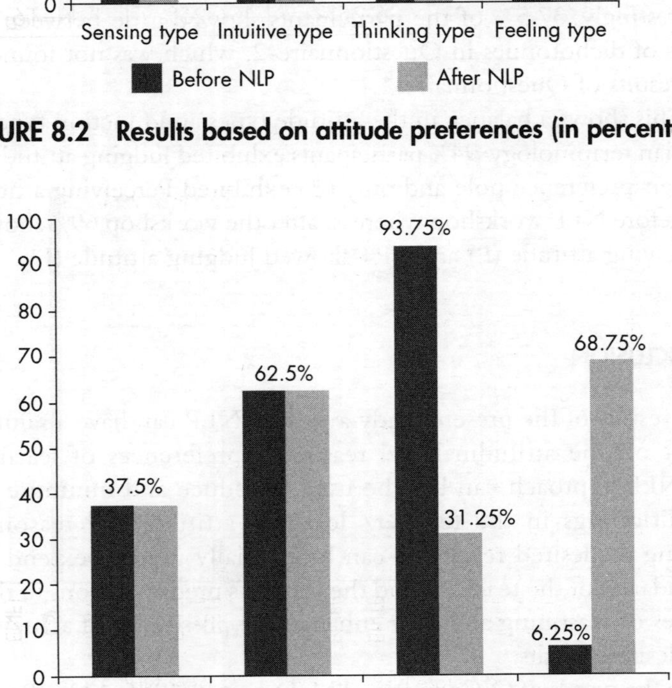

FIGURE 8.3 Results based on attitude preferences (in percentage)

NLP workshop. There was major shift from the Extrovert-Sensing-Feeling-Judging type to Extrovert-Sensing-Feeling-Perceiving type. Within the studied sample, 68.75% of the participants showed preference for the Sensing type after the NLP workshop, and of those 50% showed Extraverted-Sensing (ES) type. It is claimed that teachers and learners who have extraverted sensing as a dominant function are likely to enjoy 'learning by doing', a preference that is strongly supported in educational literature.

About 94% of the participants evinced a change in at least one preference pole. 69% of the participants showed a change in only one preference pole, whereas 25% of them showed change in two preference poles and one participant (6%) retained his earlier preference type, though the percentage differed from the first to the second questionnaire. Interestingly, 37.5% of the participants showed a tie between the poles of dichotomies in Questionnaire-2, which was not found in the results of Questionnaire-1.

This shows a balance in the attitude types and function types in Jungian terminology. 94% participants exhibited Judging attitude (J) as their preference pole and only 6% exhibited Perceiving attitude (P) before NLP workshop whereas, after the workshop 69% showed Perceiving attitude (P) and 31% showed Judging attitude (J).

Conclusion

The results of the present study aver that NLP can have a salutary effect on the attitudinal and reasoning preferences of learners. An NLP approach can best be used to reduce and minimise the conditionings in the teacher/ learner's attitude and reasoning leading to desired results. It can be crucially used to extend the boundaries of the teacher's and the learner's predispositions in their modes of reasoning and thus enhance the possibility of achieving the desired results.

In the words of O'Connor and McDermott (1996: 143), 'People respond to their map of reality and not to reality itself. We operate and communicate from those maps. Neuro-Linguistic Programming is the art of changing these maps, not reality'. It is essential for teachers to understand their own as well as the learners' maps of reality for holistic learning.

References

Andreas, Steve & Charles Faulkner (eds), (1996). *NLP: The New Technology of Achievement*. New York: Harper Collins.

Ayer, Alfred J., (1936). *Language, Truth, and Logic*. London: Gollancz. [Harmondsworth: Penguin. 2001]

Bandler, R. & J. Grinder, (1975). *The Structure of Magic: A Book about Language and Therapy*, Volume 1. Palo Alto, CA: Science and Behaviour Books.

——— (1979). *Frogs into Princes: Neurolinguistic Programming*. Boulder, CO: Real People Press.

Boroditsky, L, L. A. Schmidt & W. Phillips, (2003). 'Sex, syntax and semantics'. In D. Gentner & S. Goldin-Meadow (eds), *Language in Mind: Advances in the Study of Language and Thought*. MA: The MIT Press, 61–79.

Brown R. & E. Lenneberg, (1954). 'A study in language and cognition'. *Journal of Abnormal Social Psychology*, 49, 454–62.

Craft, Anna, (2001). 'Neuro-linguistic programming and learning theory'. *The Curriculum Journal*, 12/1, 125–36.

Dilts, Robert B. & Judith A. DeLozier, (2000). *Encyclopaedia of Systemic Neuro-Linguistic Programming and NLP New Coding*. Scotts Valley, CA: NLP University Press.

Gumperz, J. J. & S. C. Levinson, (eds), (1996). *Rethinking Linguistic Relativity*. Cambridge: Cambridge University Press.

Gupta, Anju S., (2008). 'Neuro-linguistic programming: The new kid on the block'. *Forum for Teachers of English Language and Literature*, 13, 7–9.

Horwitz, E. K., (1988). 'The beliefs about language learning of beginning university foreign language students'. *The Modern Language Journal*, 72/3, 283–94. http://blog.vcu.edu/hgsims/ Last accessed on 22 August 2016.

Kay, P. & W. Kempton, (1984). 'What is the Sapir-Whorf hypothesis?' *American Anthropologist*, 86, 65–79.

Keirsey, David & Marilyn Bates, (1984). *Please Understand Me: Character and Temperament Types*. Del Mar, CA: Prometheus Nemesis.

Knight, Sue, (2002). *NLP at work*. London: Nicholas Brealey Publishing.
Kornana, Aruna, (2012). 'Investigating the impact of language and thinking patterns on learning and teaching from the perspective of Neuro-Linguistic Programming'. M.Phil Dissertation, Jawaharlal Nehru University, New Delhi.
Korzybsky, A. (1958 [1940]) *Science and Sanity: An Introduction to Non-Aristotelian Systems and General Semantics.* Lakeville, CT: The International Non-Aristotelian Library Publishing company, The Institute of General Semantics.
Lum, C., (2001). *Scientific Thinking in Speech and Language Therapy*. Mahwah, NJ/London: Lawrence Erlbaum Associates.
Mermin, N. David, (2005). *It's About Time: Understanding Einstein's Relativity*. Princeton University Press.
Mohanan, K. P., (2011). 'A theory of crispness in banana chips: Scientific thinking in everyday life'. Pdf Ms. http: //www.iiserpune.ac.in/~mohanan/inquiry/chips.pdf
O'Connor, J. & J. Seymour, (1990). *Introducing Neuro-Linguistic Programming*. Cornwall: Aquarian Press.
Olson, D. (1977). 'From utterance to text: The bias of language in speech and writing'. *Harvard Educational Review*, 47, 257–81.
Pandey, Pramod, (2010). 'On the nature of reason in the present-day academic research'. In S. Imtiaz Hasnain & S. C. Chaudhary (eds), *Problematizing Language Studies: Cultural, Theoretical and Applied Perspectives.* New Delhi: Aakar Books, 387–97.
Pinker, Steven, (1995). *The Language Instinct*. New York: Harper Perennial Modern Classics.
——— (1997). *How the Mind Works*. New York: W. W. Norton & Company.
Quenk, N. L., (2009 [2000]). *Essentials of Myers-Briggs Type Indicator Assessment*, 2nd Edition. New York: John Wiley & Sons Inc.
Revell, J. & S. Norman, (1997). *In your hands—NLP in ELT*. London: Saffire Press.
——— (1999). *Handing Over—NLP-based Activities for Language Learning,* London: Saffire Press.
Rifkin, B., (2000). 'Revising beliefs about foreign language learning'. *Foreign Language Annals*, 33/4, 394–420.
Roderique-Davies, G., (2009). "Neuro-linguistic programming: Cargo cult psychology?". *Journal of Applied Research in Higher Education*, 1/2, 58–63.
Ryle, Gilbert, (1949). *The Concept of Mind*. London: Hutchinson University Library. [Chicago: Chicago University Press. 2002]

Sharpley, Christopher F., (1984). 'Predicate matching in NLP: A review of research on the preferred representational system'. *Journal of Counseling Psychology*, 31, 238–48.

Tosey, P. & J. Mathison, (2006). 'Introducing Neuro-linguistic programming'. Centre for Management Learning & Development, School of Management, University of Surrey.

Appendix 1
Questionnaire 1

Keirsey Temperament Sorter (KTS): Book version given before NLP workshop.

Please read the questions and options provided carefully before marking (_) the preference.

1) At a party do you:
   (a) interact with many, including strangers
   (b) interact with a few, known to you
2) Are you more:
   (a) realistic
   (b) philosophically inclined
3) Are you more intrigued by:
   (a) facts
   (b) similes
4) Are you usually more:
   (a) fair minded
   (b) kind hearted
5) Do you tend to be more:
   (a) dispassionate
   (b) sympathetic
6) Do you prefer to work:
   (a) to deadlines
   (b) just "whenever"
7) Do you tend to choose:
   (a) rather carefully
   (b) somewhat impulsively
8) At parties do you:
   (a) stay late, with increasing energy
   (b) leave early, with decreased energy
9) Are you a more:
   (a) sensible person
   (b) reflective person
10) Are you more drawn to:
   (a) hard data
   (b) abstruse ideas
11) Is it more natural for you to be:
   (a) fair to others
   (b) nice to others
12) In first approaching others are you more:
   (a) impersonal and detached
   (b) personal and engaging
13) Are you usually more:
   (a) punctual
   (b) leisurely
14) Does it bother you more having things:
   (a) incomplete
   (b) completed
15) In your social groups do you:
   (a) keep abreast of others' happenings

(b) get behind on the news

16) Are you usually more interested in:
(a) specifics
(b) concepts

17) Do you prefer writers who:
(a) say what they mean
(b) use lots of analogies

18) Are you more naturally:
(a) impartial
(b) compassionate

19) In judging are you more likely to be:
(a) impersonal
(b) sentimental

20) Do you usually:
(a) settle things
(b) keep options open

21) Are you usually rather:
(a) quick to agree to a time
(b) reluctant to agree to a time

22) In phoning do you:
(a) just start talking
(b) rehearse what you'll say

23) Facts:
(a) speak for themselves
(b) usually require interpretation

24) Do you prefer to work with:
(a) practical information
(b) abstract ideas

25) Are you inclined to be more:
(a) cool headed
(b) warm hearted

26) Would you rather be:
(a) more just than merciful
(b) more merciful than just

27) Are you more comfortable:
(a) setting a schedule
(b) putting things off

28) Are you more comfortable with:
(a) written agreements
(b) handshake agreements

29) In company do you:
(a) start conversations
(b) wait to be approached

30) Traditional common sense is:
(a) usually trustworthy
(b) often misleading

31) Children often do not:
(a) make themselves useful enough
(b) daydream enough

32) Are you usually more:
(a) tough minded
(b) tender hearted

33) Are you more:
(a) firm than gentle
(b) gentle than firm

34) Are you more prone to keep things:
(a) well organized
(b) open-ended

35) Do you put more value on the:
(a) definite
(b) variable

36) Does new interaction with others:
(a) stimulate and energize you
(b) tax your reserves

37) Are you more frequently:
(a) a practical sort of person
(b) an abstract sort of person

38) Which are you drawn to:
(a) accurate perception
(b) concept formation

39) Which is more satisfying:
(a) to discuss an issue thoroughly
(b) to arrive at agreement on an issue

40) Which rules you more:
(a) your head
(b) your heart

41) Are you more comfortable with work:
(a) contracted
(b) done on a casual basis

42) Do you prefer things to be:
(a) neat and orderly
(b) optional

43) Do you prefer:
(a) many friends with brief contact
(b) a few friends with longer contact

44) Are you more drawn to:
(a) substantial information
(b) credible assumptions

45) Are you more interested in:
(a) production
(b) research

46) Are you more comfortable when you are:
(a) objective
(b) personal

47) Do you value in yourself more that you are:
(a) unwavering
(b) devoted

48) Are you more comfortable with:
(a) final statements
(b) tentative statements

49) Are you more comfortable:
(a) after a decision
(b) before a decision

50) Do you:
(a) speak easily and at length with strangers
(b) find little to say to strangers

51) Are you usually more interested in the:
(a) particular instance
(b) general case

52) Do you feel:
(a) more practical than ingenious
(b) more ingenious than practical

53) Are you typically more a person of:
(a) clear reason
(b) strong feeling

54) Are you inclined more to be:
(a) fair-minded
(b) sympathetic

55) Is it preferable mostly to:
(a) make sure things are arranged
(b) just let things happen

56) Is it your way more to:
(a) get things settled
(b) put off settlement

57) When the phone rings do you:
(a) hasten to get to it first
(b) hope someone else will answer

58) Do you prize more in yourself a:
(a) good sense of reality
(b) good imagination

59) Are you more drawn to:
(a) fundamentals
(b) overtones

60) In judging are you usually more:
(a) neutral
(b) charitable

61) Do you consider yourself more:
(a) clear headed
(b) good willed

62) Are you more prone to:
(a) schedule events
(b) take things as they come

63) Are you the person that is more:
(a) routinized
(b) whimsical

64) Are you more inclined to be:
(a) easy to approach
(b) somewhat reserved

65) Do you have more fun with:
(a) hands-on experience
(b) blue-sky fantasy

66) In writings do you prefer:
(a) the more literal
(b) the more figurative

67) Are you usually more:
(a) unbiased
(b) compassionate

68) Are you typically more:
(a) just than lenient
(b) lenient than just

69) Is it more like you to:
(a) make snap judgments
(b) delay making judgments

70) Do you tend to be more:
(a) deliberate than spontaneous
(b) spontaneous than deliberate

Appendix 2
Questionnaire 2

Keirsey Temperament Sorter (KTS): Online version given after NLP workshop

Please read the questions and options provided carefully before marking (□) the preference.

1) I consider myself
   (a) a good conversationalist
   (b) a good listener
2) Facts
   (a) speak for themselves
   (b) illustrate principles
3) I often see
   (a) what's right in front of me
   (b) what can only be imagined
4) I feel that the greater fault is to be
   (a) too compassionate
   (b) too dispassionate
5) I'm more often
   (a) a cool-headed person
   (b) a warm-hearted person
6) When finishing a job, I like to
   (a) tie up all loose ends
   (b) move on to something else
7) I tend to
   (a) make up my mind quickly
   (b) pick and choose at some length
8) I prefer to
   (a) say right out what's on my mind
   (b) keep my ears open
9) It is worse to
   (a) have your head in the clouds
   (b) be in a rut
10) Common sense is
   (a) usually reliable
   (b) frequently questionable
11) It is better to be
   (a) just than merciful
   (b) merciful than just
12) With people I'm usually more
   (a) gentle than firm
   (b) firm than gentle
13) I'm more a kind of
   (a) serious and determined person
   (b) easy going person
14) I love to
   (a) nail things down
   (b) explore the possibilities

15) People consider me as
(a) easy to approach
(b) somewhat reserved

16) I'm a person with
(a) a strong hold on reality
(b) a vivid imagination

17) I believe that children often do not
(a) make themselves useful enough
(b) exercise their fantasy enough

18) It is worse to be
(a) a softy
(b) hard-nosed

19) I see myself as basically
(a) thick-skinned
(b) thin-skinned

20) I tend to notice
(a) disorderliness
(b) opportunities for change

21) It is preferable mostly to
(a) make sure things are arranged
(b) just let things happen naturally

22) I'm the kind of person who
(a) doesn't miss much
(b) is rather talkative

23) I prefer stories which have
(a) action and adventure
(b) fantasy and heroism

24) I tend to be more
(a) sensible than ideational
(b) ideational than sensible

25) I think of myself as a
(a) tough-minded person
(b) tender-hearted person

26) On the job, I want my activities
(a) Scheduled
(b) Unscheduled

27) I prefer agreements to be
(a) signed and sealed
(b) settled on a handshake

28) I'm inclined to be more
(a) hurried than leisurely
(b) leisurely than hurried

29) Waiting in line, I often
(a) stick to business
(b) chat with others

30) I speak more in terms of
(a) particulars than generalities
(b) generalities than particulars

31) I tend to be more
(a) factual than speculative
(b) speculative than factual

32) When in charge of others I tend to be
(a) firm and unbending
(b) forgiving and lenient

33) I'm more comfortable in making
(a) critical judgments
(b) value judgments

34) I'm more comfortable
(a) after a decision
(b) before a decision

35) Clutter in the work place is something I
(a) take time to straighten up
(b) tolerate pretty well

36) When asked to volunteer for a public event
(a) I hurry to give my name first
(b) I hope someone else will volunteer

37) I find visionaries and theorists
(a) somewhat annoying
(b) rather fascinating

38) I'm more
(a) observant than introspective
(b) introspective than observant

39) In making up my mind I'm more likely
(a) to go by data
(b) to go by desires

40) I value in myself more that I'm
(a) Reasonable
(b) devoted

41) What rules me more?
(a) my thoughts
(b) my feelings

42) I prefer to work
(a) just whenever
(b) to deadlines

43) Interacting with new people
(a) brings in lot of energy
(b) taxes my reserves

44) I'm more inclined to feel
(a) down to earth
(b) somewhat removed

45) I'm inclined to take what is said
(a) more literally
(b) more figuratively

46) What appeals to me more is
(a) consistency of thought
(b) a harmonious relationship

47) I get swayed more by
(a) convincing evidence
(b) a touching appeal

48) At work, it is more natural for me to
(a) point out mistakes
(b) try to please others

49) I usually want things
(a) settled and decided
(b) just pencilled in

50) I considered myself as
(a) an outgoing person
(b) a private person

51) I'm drawn more to
(a) fundamentals
(b) overtones

52) I'm more interested in
(a) what is actual
(b) what is possible

53) In hard circumstances, I'm sometimes
(a) too unsympathetic
(b) too sympathetic

54) In a heated discussion I
(a) stick to my guns

(b) look for common ground

55) I feel better about
(a) coming to closure
(b) keeping my options open

56) I'm more satisfied having
(a) my work in progress
(b) my work finished

57) At work I feel comfortable
(a) being sociable with my colleagues
(b) keeping more to myself

58) I'm more frequently
(a) a practical sort of person
(b) a fanciful sort of person

59) I like writers who
(a) use metaphors and symbolism
(b) say what they mean

60) I take it as a compliment if someone says
(a) I'm a logical person
(b) I'm a sentimental person

61) I wish more for myself,
(a) strength of will
(b) strength of emotion

62) In most situations I'm more
(a) deliberate than spontaneous
(b) spontaneous than deliberate

63) I'm very
(a) routinized
(b) unpredictable

64) At a party, I love to
(a) interact with different people, even strangers
(b) interact only with my friends

65) I'm more likely to trust
(a) my experiences
(b) my ideas

66) It is easier for me to
(a) put others to good use
(b) identify with others

67) People can disappoint me by being
(a) warm and considerate
(b) frank and straightforward

68) In sizing up others, I tend to be
(a) friendly and personal
(b) objective and impersonal

69) I tend to choose
(a) rather carefully
(b) somewhat impulsively

70) I more often prefer
a) final unaltered statements
b) tentative preliminary statements

Appendix 3

Evaluation Table for Questionnaire 1 and 2

	E1	I1		S1	N1		S2	N2		T1	F1		T2	F2		J1	P1		J2	P2
	a	b		a	b		a	b		a	b		a	b		a	b		a	b
1			2			3			4			5			6			7		
8			9			10			11			12			13			14		
15			16			17			18			19			20			21		
22			23			24			25			26			27			28		
29			30			31			32			33			34			35		
36			37			38			39			40			41			42		
43			44			45			46			47			48			49		
50			51			52			53			54			55			56		
57			58			59			60			61			62			63		
64			65			66			67			68			69			70		
			3	S1	N1 4	3	S2	N2 4	5	T1	F1 6	5	T2	F2 6	7	J1	P1 8	7	J2	P2 8

	S1 +S2 / N1 +N2	T1 +T2 / F1 +F2	J1 +J2 / P1 +P2
1 E / I 2	3 S / N 4	5 T / F 6	7 J / P 8

Steps to determine the typology

1. Transfer the answer from the test sheet to the answer sheet below. (put 'X' in the 'a' or 'b' box for each number)
2. Add the number of times 'X' occurs in each column and enter the total in the box directly below the associated column.
3. All totals with the same letters should be added together to form the new letter total. (ex: S1+S2=S)
4. Circle the highest value for each pair of letters. (ex: E or I, S or N, T or F, J or P)
5. The resulting 4 letters represent the typology.

CHAPTER 9

Reformulation as a Technique for Teaching Writing

YASMEEN LUKMANI AND B. SAMAL

Abstract

Writing skills in the process of learning a second language involve mainly the learning of the grammar of the language, and the use of the skills of cohesion and coherence in the formulation of text. Teaching practice in India concentrates practically only on the acquisition of grammar, in spite of the fact that language acquisition studies have conclusively established that there is a specific learning agenda in the learner's mind as he/ she is exposed to the flow of language. What is taught is not usually automatically learnt. Following from this approach, in the teaching experiment that is reported here conducted to teach writing, no attempt is made to teach grammar explicitly, instead, the process of 'reformulation' is followed. Here, instead of correcting the writing efforts of the whole class, a representative script is selected which is edited to read as well as could be expected of that level of student. The original and edited scripts are compared in the next class session by the whole class. In the session after this, students write again on the same topic, producing the 'rewritten' script. This is the procedure followed. In the course of the 3-month period of the experiment, the students of the Experimental Group showed improvement over the Control Group in their overall writing ability from pre-test to post-test, and specifically in the aspect of coherence.

Introduction

The aim of this study is to investigate the usefulness of the 'Reformulation' Technique (Allwright 1984: 1988) in improving writing abilities. The principle of this reformulation technique is far removed from the notion of recasting sentences in order to correct for error, in particular, errors looked at in isolation within a specific sentence, which is the normal treatment meted out to students trying to improve their written English. This constitutes input to the learner which is pre-emptive/ preventive/ pre-decided, i.e. basically what the grammar books put down as the norms of correct English, and not what learners are actually in a position to absorb at that moment, or which helps to bring out the meaning they wish to convey.

The approach being put forward here, in contrast, is responsive input, that is, responsive both in content (those things which the learner's formulation lacks) and in context (when the learner has actually grappled with a formulation). Instead of pointing out the error, this technique tries to fill out and complete the meaning the student is trying to convey by using the appropriate conventions of written language, whether in terms of grammar (sentence-based), cohesion (linking together statements or sentences with appropriate transitions, including cohesive links: a text-based activity) or coherence (appropriate organisation of ideas, connectedness and logical development, which is also text-based activity). An appropriately reformulated version is created from an original student script, in order to introduce improvements in formulation that are possible in the text as a whole, and further, to lead the students into producing another draft, or a 'rewritten' version, without reference to the original draft. It is expected that this new draft, written solely by the student, will be qualitatively much better than the original, and thus, indicate that genuine learning has taken place.

Reformulation Technique

The Reformulation Technique involves all students writing on a particular topic, and before the next class, the teacher has chosen a 'representative' script, i.e. one representative of the average level of student production in that class, which she then reformulates, according to the approach outlined above, for the benefit of the entire class. The reformulated version and the original, on which this is based, could then be discussed by the whole class. (This could be done by writing up both attempts on two blackboards, or showing them side by side on a projector or by providing photocopies to the students.) The process of comparing the two can lead to a co-operative classroom atmosphere, where the students can discover for themselves important aspects relating to the organisation of ideas and language required to express themselves in writing. It must be borne in mind that the teacher is only trying to improve the script to the level to which the student can reasonably be expected to reach: an ideal version is not aimed at.

In order to test whether student writing would improve if they are taught through the reformulation technique, an experiment was conducted in which two reasonably matched groups of students were taken who were both to be trained in writing skills: the Experimental Group to be given the experimental treatment of Reformulation (exclusively) and the other, the Control Group, to be given the normal content of a writing class, which among other things involves the teacher correcting student production. The subjects of the present study were students of Commerce in their first year of undergraduate study at a college affiliated to the University of Bombay. It was conducted in the class period of a regular course of study, namely, Business Communication, so the types of writing tasks used were those that were required in their regular course syllabus.

It was hypothesised that:

> Training in writing through the use of the reformulation technique would lead to improved writing ability, namely, the ability to produce grammatically correct, cohesive and coherent texts, as judged by an English teacher and a subject teacher of Commerce.

Method

Subjects

Two groups of 30 students, each belonging to the First Year B. Com Class of a representative College of Commerce and Economics, at the University of Bombay, who were studying Business Communication as one of their courses, formed the Experimental and Control Groups. The batches could not be formed on the basis of student performance on a proficiency test in English because this was not feasible in the set-up. Instead, the regular tutorial batches of the class to which students had been randomly assigned were used for the purpose. This meant that the entry level of the two groups could not be matched exactly. One set of two groups was used and then abandoned because of disparities in entry level proficiency (on the basis of a written exercise). Another set of two groups was then selected which showed less disparity. As yet another set of groups would not be readily available, it was decided to use these. The two groups were considered to be reasonably well-matched. However, in order to avoid the charge of manipulating the results, the group which performed better at entry point was used as the Control Group, while the other constituted the Experimental Group. Later, however, when the statistical analysis was done, it was found that the initial difference between the Experimental and Control Groups was actually significant at the .05 level of significance, with the Control Group having the advantage.

Experimenter

One of the researchers, a regular teacher at the college, and hence known to the students, conducted the sessions for both the Experimental and Control Groups. The scripts were assessed by both the researcher (an English teacher) and a subject teacher of Commerce.

Materials and procedures

The writing exercises that were set were based on the Business Communication syllabus of the University of Bombay and gave practice in writing expository prose. These consisted of the following and were used in the Experiment: writing of paragraphs (Exercises I, II and VII), a speech (Exercise III), a report (Exercise IV), a circular (Exercise V), and a representation regarding a problem

(Exercise VI). These exercises were done as part of the regular writing assignments of the students at their tutorial sessions. The Business Communication course was of a year's duration, but the experimental treatment was given for one term only, that is, for three and a half months.

The exercise that was used to match the two groups was counted as Exercise I and was assessed by both a subject teacher as well as the experimenter. This was considered to mark the starting level of the students for the purposes of this experiment. Exercise VII, which was the terminal exercise, was also assessed by both the experimenter and the same subject teacher.

Results

The results indicate that there has been a statistically significant improvement in both the Experimental and Control Groups from Exercise I to VII (see Table 9.1). Some progress in academic development is expected in the course of a term, whatever the method of teaching, so the Control Group is also expected to have improved to some extent.

TABLE 9.1 Performance of the Experimental Group (original scripts) (EO) Experimental Group (rewritten versions) (ER) and Control Group (C)

Group	Ex I		Ex VII		t-value
	Mean Scores	S.D.	Mean Scores	S.D.	
EO	2.37	1.25	3.93	0.84	6.10**
Er	2.90	0.83	4.37	0.74	7.97**
C	2.87	0.84	8.93	0.67	6.44**

* $p < 0.001$

EO = Experimental Group (Original Script)

As noted earlier, the proficiency of the Experimental and Control Groups was considerably different at entry point because it was not possible to match the groups further within the regular college set-up.

The level of difference showed a trend towards significance (t-value 1.78; $p<.05$), with the Control Group showing superiority. At the terminal point (Exercise VII), however, both groups got identical scores. This indicates that the improvement over the course of the experiment for the Experimental Group was much greater than the corresponding improvement for the Control Group, indicating that reformulation as a technique for the teaching of writing had, been successful.

Table 9.2 shows the improvement from Exercise I to Exercise VII in terms of percentages. The improvement for the Experimental Group (original scripts) was 65.82%; for the rewritten version of the Experimental Group it was 50.69% and for the Control Group it was 36.93 %. This indicates the much greater extent to which the Experimental Group has improved. The table is given below.

TABLE 9.2 Improvement in scores from Exercise I to VII in the Experimental Group Original Script, Experimental Group Rewritten Version and Control Group: Original Script

Group	Improvement in Scores Ex I–Ex VII	Improvement in Scores (% age) Ex I–Ex VII
EO	1.56	65.82
ER	1.47	50–69
C	1.06	36.93

EO = Experimental Group (Original Script)
ER = Experimental Group (Rewritten Script)
C = Control Group.

Analysis of Experimental Group Scripts

In order to give a flavour of the nature of the learning that was taking place for the Experimental Group, given below is the representative script chosen for Exercise I (out of the scripts produced) and its reformulated version, as well as the representative script for Exercise VII (out of the original scripts produced) and its reformulated version. The nature of the differences between each set of scripts is then analysed. For lack of space, the Control Group scripts will not be discussed.

Exercise I: Representative script (original) of the Experimental Group

(S1) Education has certain aims and objectives. (S2) The purpose of education is to prepare children for a full and active life. (S3) Free education cannot bring any solution for this purpose. (S4) Education itself cannot solve the problems of our society. (S5) For instance, unemployed graduates dislike the idea of physical labour. (S6) Therefore, they are useless members of the society. (S7) True education makes people realise the value of physical work. (S8) We can do without professor but we cannot do without farmers. (S9) Education that teaches us the dignity of labour is really valuable. (S10) It must teach people to do whatever job is suitable to their intelligence and capability.

Exercise I: Reformulated version

(S1) Education has certain aims and objectives. (S2) The purpose of education is to prepare children for a full and active life. (S3) Education must be related to our life and our problems, particularly social problems. (S4) True education can make people realise that physical work is not low and despicable. (S5) Unemployed graduates need not feel that they are sinking very low if they turn to physical labour for an occupation. (S6) Additionally, it must not be forgotten that while we can do without professors, we cannot do without farmers. (S7) Education has, unfortunately, created graduates who dislike the idea of physical labour. (S8) True education should make people realise the value of both physical and mental work. (S9) It should teach people to do whatever job is best suited to their intelligence and capabilities.

Analysis

The first two lines of the reformulated version, namely, S1 and S2, remain the same as in the original. S3, which does not occur in the original script, is added to connect the notion of education to its relationship with social problems. In the original script, there are no such connecting statements. S4 (reformulated) takes over S7 of the original script and expands it by adding that 'physical work is not low and despicable'. This expansion is required in order to bring out the relationship between 'physical work' and 'the dignity of labour' mentioned in the original. S5 (reformulated) is taken from S5 (original) and elaborated. The idea was lost in the original script because of wrong placement. S6 (reformulated) brings in S8 (original) with the connecting words: 'Additionally, it must not be forgotten that while...' these additions indicate that a new point, related to the same one, is being made. S7 (reformulated) takes over S7 (original), with the difference that in the original it is a statement of fact, whereas in the reformulated version it becomes 'should'. S9 (reformulated) is essentially the same as S10 (original). Both these are the closing statements of the two versions.

As seen above, the opening and closing lines in the reformulated versions have not been changed. Connections have, however, been established between the different parts of the argument in the body of the paragraph. In the original version, the student has not been able to connect related ideas. Paragraph 1 seems more or less parallel to paragraph 2, with each having a general statement leading to basically the same thought in both. Instead of repeating the same kind of information in the two paragraphs, related ideas have been brought together and properly divided between the two paragraphs.

Exercise VII: Representative script (original) of Experimental Group

(S1) The present system under which some countries one cannot apply for a post even as a clerk unless one is a graduate. (S2) Many enter college, not out of love of learning, but because they need a degree to get a job. (S3) Such concern for job prospect destroys the enjoyment of the study themselves. (S4) The highest ambition of the majority of college students in one such country is to get jobs such as assistance in government offices. (S5) It is a sad thing that from the beginning they do not aim higher. (S6) But if this is so the greater part of their university studies is totally unreal and irrelevant. (S7) Many of these students must see their studies as a waste of time, but they have to complete them for getting a job.

Exercise VII: Reformulated version

(S1) Under the present system in our country, one cannot apply for a post even as a clerk, unless one is a graduate. (S2) Many students, therefore, enter college not out of a love for learning, but because they need a degree to get a job. (S3) Such concern for actual job prospects may prevent them from getting the most out of their studies. (S4) At the same time, students very often seem to aim no higher than getting jobs as assistants in government offices. (S5) It is sad that from the outset, their ambition is so limited. (S6) If these factors are, in fact, true, the greater part of University education must appear unreal and irrelevant to them. (S7) Indeed, many of these students must see their studies as a waste of time, but nevertheless, have to complete them to be sure of getting employment.

Analysis

In Exercise VII, the representative script shows a marked improvement over the representative script of Exercise I. The problem in Exercise I is mainly that of coherence, a more serious error than the problems in Exercise VII, which relate mainly to grammar and cohesion. The ideas do not require reorganisation as in Exercise I, for sentences occur in the same order in the reformulated version, albeit with some internal changes.

In S1 (original), the phrase 'under which' suggesting the beginning of a subordinate clause is deceptive because no such clause follows. This is a grammatical error and has been removed in the reformulated version. In S1 (original) 'one such country' has been changed to 'our country', in order to make the reference more specific. In S2 (reformulated) the word 'therefore' has been inserted to make the connection between the sentences more clear. S3 (original) has been partially reworked for greater stylistic felicity. It is made more tentative by adding words such as 'very often' and '*seem* to aim'. In the original, the statement was a bit too strong. In S4 (reformulated) the word 'again' is used to indicate that one more reason is being provided. S3 and S4 now appear more clearly as two separate reasons for S2. S5 is only a stylistic improvement on the original. In S6 (original), again, the statement is unnecessarily strong, 'totally unreal and irrelevant'. In S7, the words 'indeed' and 'nevertheless' have been inserted in order to add the proper cohesive links; while 'getting employment' replaces 'getting a job' because it sounds less casual and informal, and is better suited to a serious piece of writing.

The qualitative analysis shows that the main improvement in the Experimental Group from Exercise I to VII is in the area of coherence, while problems of grammar and cohesion remain relatively unchanged. It is argued that errors of coherence are more crucial, because they can disrupt meaning, and so, improvement in this area indicates that students are better able to get a clear and unambiguous meaning across. In any case, much grammatical improvement is not possible within three months.

It can be seen that on many occasions both the Experimental and Control Groups fail to use the appropriate cohesive devices, so their ideas are neither presented clearly, nor is there a smooth flow to their writing. It is felt that cohesion is an area which needs greater attention. Among the grammatical errors produced, prominent is the absence of ability to divide sentences into appropriate clauses; they lack control over complex sentences, producing short, abrupt sentences in places where the ideas could have been better connected by subordinating some of these sentences.

The study pinpoints the need to make teaching methodology take coherence and cohesion much more seriously than they do, in the teaching of writing. Instead of focusing on sentential grammar, which in spite of the teacher's best efforts, hardly shows perceptible improvement in our classrooms, features of discourse, such as coherence and cohesion, should be emphasised. Grammar is a matter of the learning agenda unfolding in the mind of the child, as language acquisition studies have very clearly established, and whether in the child or older learner, this cannot be hurried by the process of teaching. Grammar will take its own time, and we know that children learning their first language take several years to learn correct sentence grammar. Providing practice in writing, making it seem relevant and meaningful, and insisting on issues of clarity and of making sense, will help to eventually acquire the correct grammatical forms, *without explicit attention to grammatical features.*

The experiment described above shows how much progress can be made in producing meaningful written language by using the Reformulation Technique, particularly when it is linked with a focus on the primacy of coherence and cohesion in learning to write. This technique is suggested as a practical, easy-to-implement and effective method for teachers to use in the classroom.

References

Allwright, R. L., (1984). 'Don't correct—reformulate'. Paper presented at TESOL, Houston, Texas: Mimeo.

Allwright, R. L., M. F. Woodley, & J. M. Allwright, (1988). 'Investigating reformulation as a practical strategy for the teaching of academic writing'. *Applied Linguistics*, 9/ 3, 236–56.

Samel, B., (1989). 'Reformulation as a technique for teaching writing (a discourse perspective)'. Unpublished M.Phil dissertation. University of Bombay.

CHAPTER 10

Karaoke: A Powerful Tool to Improve Reading Skills

AARTI M. PUNJABI AND YASMEEN LUKMANI

Abstract

Huge literacy projects have been set up by Brij Kothari and others following in his wake, using the moving picture with songs or other material accompanied by the words spoken being written on the screen in the same language (Same Language Subtitling). The success of these projects prompted the decision to try out the technique to improve reading skills in English with young children, making use of the same principles as Same Language Subtitling (SLS), but in a smaller through the of karaoke. Songs were sung by the students as a group, with the words appearing on the moving strip. It was expected that this simple, enjoyable exercise would give rise to improvement in reading speed and reading comprehension (both literal and inferential skills being tested). The tests were task-oriented exercises, inspired by the work of N. S. Prabhu, which forced the students to think hard and creatively to produce the answers. Some examples of the songs used and the tasks devised are given.

The experiment presented here was inspired by the work of Brij Kothari of the Indian Institute of Management, Ahmedabad and others (2002, 2004) when he used 'Same Language Subtitling' (SLS) to improve functional literacy rates in India, whether within the school system or on adults outside the classroom. In 1999, he experimented with subtitles on Chitrageet, a Gujarati television programme; in 2002, the Doordarshan network subtitled (in Hindi) their national programme Chitrahaar (now called Rangoli), while since 2006, SLS has been implemented on a weekly programme each in Hindi, Bengali, Gujarati, Punjabi, Kannada, Telugu, Tamil, and Marathi, i.e., karaoke-style subtitles on popular songs on television. This gives the viewers an opportunity to sing along with the songs in the programme. While doing this, they begin paying attention to the moving strip with the lines of the lyrics at the bottom of the screen. Often, they copy the words on paper, going back to them after the show was over. By dint of hearing songs they like, and singing along with them, they unconsciously absorb the graphic form of the words which are before them on the screen. At the end of a given time frame, a significant proportion of these audiences have been found to move from being illiterate or neo-literate to literate, painlessly, and in a short period of time.

In the Indian school system, effective literacy, it appears, from the research done by Kothari and others, is hard to achieve. Even after completing Grade 5, or primary schooling, only 11% become literate. 71% achieve properly literate only low levels of literacy and 18% remain completely illiterate. However, almost anyone who has completed at least one year of schooling is reported as 'literate' when the census is conducted.

Kothari's team looked at the impact of SLS on school children who were illiterate in 2002, when SLS was used on the Rangoli programme. Without any exposure to SLS, the team found that 24% of the children became good readers after five years of schooling; however, from the school children exposed to SLS, 56% became good readers.

The impact of SLS on adult illiterates was similar to that on children, although it was less pronounced. After five years, only 3% illiterate adults became good readers in the non-SLS group; in the SLS group, 12% became good readers.

Further, it was found that among self-professed 'literates', five years of SLS exposure resulted in newspaper reading at least once a week, going up from 42% to 70%.

Kothari is the president of Planet Read, a non-profit organisation involved in furthering Same Language Subtitling throughout the world. He is also the founder of Book Box, a social venture funded by First Light Ventures that produces animated, read-along stories for children in languages such as English, Spanish, Mandarin, Hindi, and over twenty-one others.

Going by the success of this project, an attempt was made by the researchers to do something on the same general lines to improve the reading skills of students. In place of television, it was decided to use karaoke, a form of interactive entertainment, using pop songs which the learners sang along with the recorded music, while looking at the lyrics displayed on a video screen. Using only an ordinary screen and a microphone karaoke was a fun approach to linking words with sounds. By means of a moving symbol, or changes in colour and video images, the singers would be guided to the actual words being sung. Actually SLS provided them with more than an opportunity to sing; it helped them get at some of the words/ lines they were not clear about in the songs they already knew. This was an added incentive to read the SLS.

Music is one of the ways in which the level of motivation to learn is raised. It has been reported that music, even in contexts quite removed from SLS, helps second language learners acquire vocabulary and grammar, improve spelling and develop their abilities in reading, writing, speaking and listening (Jolly 1975; Martin 1983; Mitchell 1983; Jalongo & Bromley 1984).

Psycholinguistic research has also shown that during an electroencephalogram (ECG), music can change the nature of brainwaves and make the mind more receptive to learning. Brain functioning improves and more complex thinking and learning ensues (Davies 2000).

Medina (2002) says that the frequent singing of songs gives learners familiarity with the words used, so their confidence level regarding language use rises. Furthermore, by engaging in a pleasurable experience, they are relaxed, their inhibitions lowered, and yet, simultaneously, by being more attentive than usual, they are more receptive to learning. Again, through songs, students are exposed to 'authentic' examples of the second language/ target vocabulary and grammar, so linguistic routines and grammatical patterns are moulded in context.

The current study, based on these principles, was done on school-going children of the age group 10.5–11.5 years, drawn from classes 5 and 6 of three English-medium schools following the ICSE curriculum. They could, at entry level, read simple sentences, recognise the emotions behind the text and identify simple grammatical structures. The study concerns itself with the effect of karaoke on increasing their reading speed, and improving their reading skills by enhancing their ability to get at literal and inferential meaning more efficiently. Going by the basic principle, well-established in psycholinguistic and language learning theory since the 1970s, that language is acquired interactively in context rather than consciously learned through drilling in grammatical rules (see Prabhu 1987), it was believed that introducing fun into the classroom and greater interactivity would take the pressure off the learning process, and provide a major form of motivation to engage with the language.

While karaoke has been seen to work with literacy issues, the process of reading also involves more complex skills. It was felt that to improve reading comprehension at both the literal and inferential levels, suitable instructional practices had to be incorporated in the experiment. In order to be effective, these exercises must ultimately be fun-filled, and teaching methodology made to draw on the approved principles of language acquisition theory, and the principles of psychological receptivity. The activities used in this experiment all fell into the category of 'task-based learning'. Prabhu (1987: 24) defines a task as 'an activity which required learners to arrive at an outcome from given information through some process of thought, and which allowed teachers to control and regulate the process.' He argued that the process must focus on the improvement of meaning transmission rather than the acquisition of form. This is the natural process of learning any child goes through outside the classroom, and through the concentration on meaningfulness in activities, strangely enough, form gets acquired, almost as a side product, alongside normal (and pleasurable) communication. It is only with the school system with its heavily Calvinistic principles of making children learn through hard work and through the learning of difficult items, sitting for long hours and doing things they do not enjoy, that learning becomes a problem.

Thus, tasks, Prabhu claims, can engage the mind and interests of children and can make learning a natural and spontaneous activity. Prabhu had tried out his intuitive ideas on teaching English to school children living in slums in Bangalore and then Madras, making the classes rollicking fun and getting the children to use English in speech and writing. These ideas took some time to crystallise and for him to develop his procedural syllabus, which was a set of procedures, or tasks, for learning. As a result, before Prabhu was able to bring out his own definitive book on the subject, his ideas attracting much international attention, were floating in the world of Applied Linguistics and the sense of involvement and excitement in the honing of these ideas had a number of scholars bring out books on the subject. The result was that their names got associated with the idea of task-oriented language teaching, more so, perhaps than that of Prabhu, who had not only initiated the idea, but done the major work in trialling such a project.

The current work drawing its inspiration from the work of both Kothari and Prabhu is now presented. A small-scale exploratory experiment was conducted in the researcher's house (for want of a better place having all the required facilities) to test whether karaoke improved the reading skills of students, in terms of reading speed, and reading comprehension, involving both literal and inferential skills. The students were drawn from classes 5 and 6 from three different schools. A screening test (which was later considered as the pre-test) showed that a fair number of these students were linguistically at the same level. Eighteen students were randomly selected, and from this, and two groups, the Experimental and Control Groups, were formed consisting of nine students each. The Experimental Group met for a total of eight sessions of forty-five minutes each. The sessions consisted of singing songs with the aid of karaoke, with a few task-oriented exercises based on the songs. The Control Group also met for the same amount of time but was only given reading comprehension exercises to do individually, with no interaction among the students. They thus had a great deal of more individual practice in reading comprehension than the Experimental Group.

Samples of Activities

The emphasis on task-orientedness led to devising a number of activities along with each karaoke song. Some tasks set on the songs in two of the sessions are given below as examples.

Activities Conducted in Session 5 of the Course

The Experimental Group students were divided into two sub-groups and each group sang 'Rudolph the Red-Nosed Reindeer' twice. They were asked to pay attention to the lyric, as they would be asked questions on the song. The nature of the questions is given in brackets. These labels will become clear in the next section.

Activity 1

A worksheet was given which had to be answered individually, in writing. When they finished reading the questions, the song was played again. They then had ten minutes to answer the questions. A sample of the questions asked and the question types is listed below.

1. Name all the reindeer mentioned. (Factual: Low)
2. What do these phrases mean 'call names'; 'go down in history'? (Factual: Medium)
3. Why did the reindeer call Rudolph names? (Inferential: Medium)
4. Find words from the song that are closest in meaning to the following: 'happy', 'remember'. (Factual: Medium)
5. Write two synonyms for the word 'shiny'. (Factual: High)

Activity 2

The students were divided into groups of three. The song 'Yellow Submarine' was played again and they had to make a list of words beginning with the letters S and L from the song. Each group then drew a submarine and wrote a list of the words from the song they associated with it. The lists were then read aloud.

Activities Conducted in Session 6

The students were divided into two groups. The songs played were, 'Rudolph the Red-Nosed Reindeer' and 'Dashing through the Snow'. Each group sang both the songs.

Activity 1

The lyrics of both the songs were written on slips of paper— three words on each slip; these slips were then jumbled. Each group worked separately to get the songs in correct order. The first group to do so was declared the winner. In the meantime, the songs were being played in the background.

Activity 2

They were asked to do the following:

Find a word each from the lyrics for the following words/ phrases (Factual: High)

A group of musicians
Covered entrance to a building
Option
Appear

Both groups were given a test of reading speed at the pre-test and post-test. They were also given a test of reading comprehension, consisting of an unseen passage raising discursive ideas, with questions. The questions demanded both Literal and Inferential skills, with three levels of difficulty—Low, Middle and High. Literal questions were, by and large, factual, and did not require a great deal of search in the passage for the answer. Inferential questions included a large number of categories, including analysis, synthesis, interpretation, argument and inference proper, and the answer might involve looking at various parts of the passage. In practice, it becomes very difficult to distinguish, in a principled way, between all these categories, so here they were all clubbed together under the category 'inferential'. This format had been used successfully in the

Course Evaluation of the Communication Skills course In English, run at the First Year BA of the colleges of Mumbai University. (Lukmani et al. 1988)

The nature of the passages at the pre-and post-tests were very similar and yielded the same number of factual and inferential questions. Given below is the post-test passage to give an idea of the nature of the passages and questions on them. For lack of space, the pre-test is not given.

Post-test Passage

Mosaic is a piece of work in which a pattern is produced by putting together small pieces of differently coloured marble, glass, or stone pieces. Together, the pieces form a picture pattern to make a decorative art form. It was used to decorate the interiors of houses.

It is difficult to say exactly where this art originated, as several different civilisations, not connected with each other, produced it around the same time. Some think that the Greeks were the first to create mosaic art some 5000 years ago. For centuries they searched for coloured pebbles and stones in river beds and seashores to decorate their mud houses. Later, the rich decorated the floors of their mansions with big slabs of contrasting coloured stones. It was the Greeks who gradually turned it into an art form, making beautiful geometric patterns and detailed scenes of people and animals.

The Romans followed the Greeks, and used mosaic to decorate everything from floors in their homes to their churches. In ancient times, a skilled craftsman would lay about 200 stones an hour to make an intricate design, taking several months to complete an entire floor. That is why the mosaics became a mark of the wealthy. The Romans loved to picture their gods in their mosaics and also make geometric designs.

From the 5thC onwards, the Byzantine Empire in popularized the art even further. Their mosaics were different from those of the Romans in that the latter used this mostly on their floors, whereas the Byzantines used it to decorate their walls as well. They used a special glass smalti which was made from thick sheets of coloured glass. Smalti was sometimes backed with reflective gold or silver leaf. The beauty of smalti was that it allowed the light to reflect within the glass and the gold and silver backing sparkled as *the viewer looked at it from different angles. The Byzantines used similar themes as the Romans, but added pictures of emperors and empresses.*

These days one can create a mosaic pattern within seconds on the computer.

Given below are the questions, with the expected answer, and analysis of the skills required to answer them.

Questions

Q 1: What was the purpose of using mosaic? (Factual: Low)
A: To decorate the interiors of homes.
[Analysis: The answer is found in one place; the degree of search is limited. But some thinking is involved, as the answer to the first question is not found automatically in the first line of the passage, as is the case with most reading comprehension questions.]

Q 2: Find a word from the passage that means the same as the word 'slowly'. (Factual: Medium)
A: gradually (end of paragraph 2).
[Analysis: The operation is factual, but nevertheless required searching the whole passage for the answer; hence it is considered to be of medium difficulty.]

Q 3: Do we know where mosaic art began? Which sentence/ words can you quote from the text in support of your answer? (Inference: Low)
A: No, it is not clearly stated. The words supporting this conclusion are: 'It is difficult to say exactly where this art originated, as several different civilisations, not connected with each other produced their own mosaic art around the same time. Some think that the Greeks were the first ….'
[Analysis: The answer is clearly stated in one place in the text, but it nevertheless requires some inference, as the words used in the question are quite different from those in the text, and also it is not factual matter that is being dealt with, but one of interpretation.]

Q 4: Technology has made mosaic art simpler. How? (Inference: Medium)
A: Computers can create mosaic patterns within seconds.
[Analysis: An association has to be made between technology and

computers, which is an inference. It is of medium difficulty as the answer is found in one sentence, and as technology is connected with today or 'these days'. Moreover, it comes at the end of the passage, and the passage is ordered chronologically, so the expectation is that it is the most recent development.]

Q 5: List any one similarity and one difference between the way the Greeks and the Romans used mosaic art. (Inference: High)
A: Similarity: Use of geometric patterns.
Difference: The Greeks focused on people and animals, while the Romans loved to present their gods in mosaic art.
[Analysis: The answer involves finding instances of similarity and difference which requires powers of abstraction. The answer has also to be put together from two different paragraphs.]

Results of the experiment

The results of the experiment are given below in the tables.

TABLE 10.1 Comparison of pre-test and post-test scores on reading comprehension

	Pre-test			Post-test				
	Marks	Mean Scores	S.D	Marks	Mean Scores	S.D	t-value	Sig
Experimental Group	78	8.6	4.14	102	11.3	3.25	1.58	n.s.
Control Group	66.5	7.38	3.54	79.5	8.83	3.18	0.94	n.s.

TABLE 10.2 Gains from pre-test to post-test for all questions

	Pre-Test Marks	Pre-Test Mean Scores	Post-Test Marks	Post-Test Mean Scores	Gains in Mean Scores	Percentage of Increases
Experimental Group	78	8.6	102	11.33	2.73	13.65%
Control Group	66.5	7.38	79.5	8.83	1.45	7.25%

TABLE 10.3 Gains from pre-test to post-test for factual and inferential questions

	Pre-Test Mean Scores		Post-Test Mean Scores		Gains from Pre-Test to Post-Test	
	Factual	Inferential	Factual	Inferential	Factual	Inferential
Experimental Group	6.8	2.5	6.9	3.5	0.1	1.0
Control Group	5.6	1.9	6.3	2.3	0.7	0.4

TABLE 10.4 Reading speed at the pre-test and post-test levels

	Pre-Test		Post-Test		Gains	
	Total WPM *	Mean Scores	Total WPM	Mean Scores	Total	Mean Scores
Experimental Group	826.16	91.79	939.01	104.33	112.85	12.56
Control Group	875.77	97.30	919.76	102.19	43.99	4.89

*WPM= Words per minute

As the number of students was so small and the sessions so limited, nothing has emerged of statistical significance. This is to be expected as the experiment was exploratory in nature. However, it indicates that the Experimental Group shows a trend towards improvement greater than the Control Group in all aspects. Their reading speed has improved dramatically and their ability to answer inferential questions has also improved a great deal. The behaviour of the students was another indication. They were so happy with the sessions that they were reluctant to leave and begged the researcher to hold more such sessions.

References

Davies, N. L., (2000). 'Learning …the beat goes on'. *Childhood Education.*148–53.

Jalongo, M. & K. Bromley, (1984). 'Developing linguistic competence through song'. *Reading Teacher,* 37/9, 840–45.

Jolly, Y., (1975). 'The use of songs in teaching foreign languages'. *Modern Language Journal*, 59/1, 11–14.

Kothari, B., J. Takeda, A. Joshi, & A. Pandey, (2002). 'Same language subtitling: A butterfly for literacy?' *International Journal of Lifelong Education*, 21/1, 55–66.

Kothari, Brij, Avinash Pandey, & Amita Chudgar, (2004). 'Reading out of the "idiot box": Same-language subtitling on television in India'. *Information Technologies and International Development*, 2/1, 23–44.

Lukmani, Y., A. Davies, V. Balaporia, M. Colaco, (1995). 'Course evaluation of "communicational skills in English": A report'. Unpublished report presented to the University of Bombay and the British Council, 1988. Published as 'Evaluation of a mainstream communicative course'. In (eds) R. K. Agniotri and A. L. Khanna, *English Language Teaching, Research in Applied Linguistics, 2*, Sage, N. Delhi,.

Martin, M., (1983). 'Success! Teaching spelling with music'. *Academic Therapy*, 18/4, 505–06.

Medina, S. 'Using music to enhance second language acquisition: From theory to practice'. In Lalas, J. & Lee, S. 2002.Mitchell, M. "Aerobic ESL: Variations on a total physical response theme" *TESL Reporter, 16*, 1983: 23–27.

Prabhu, N. S. (1987). *Second Language Pedagogy*. Oxford: Oxford University Press.

www.planetread.com. Accessed on 18 June 2009.

Punjabi, Aarti, M. (2012). 'Karaoke: A powerful tool to improve reading skills'. Unpublished M.Phil dissertation. University of Mumbai.

Appendix: Songs Used In Activities

JINGLE BELLS

Dashing through the snow
In a one horse open sleigh
O'er the fields we go
Laughing all the way
Bells on bob tails ring
Making spirits bright
What fun it is to laugh and sing
A sleighing song tonight

Oh, jingle bells, jingle bells
Jingle all the way
Oh, what fun it is to ride
In a one horse open sleigh
Jingle bells, jingle bells
Jingle all the way
Oh, what fun it is to ride
In a one horse open sleigh

A day or two ago
I thought I'd take a ride
And soon Miss Fanny Bright
Was seated by my side
The horse was lean and lank
Misfortune seemed his lot
We got into a drifted bank
And then we got upsot

Oh, jingle bells, jingle bells
Jingle all the way
Oh, what fun it is to ride
In a one horse open sleigh
Jingle bells, jingle bells

Jingle all the way
Oh, what fun it is to ride
In a one horse open sleigh yeah

Jingle bells, jingle bells
Jingle all the way
Oh, what fun it is to ride
In a one horse open sleigh
Jingle bells, jingle bells
Jingle all the way
Oh, what fun it is to ride
In a one horse open sleigh

RUDOLPH THE RED-NOSED REINDEER

Rudolph the Red-Nosed Reindeer
Had a very shiny nose,
And if you ever saw it,
You would even say it glows. Like a light bulb!
All of the other reindeer
Used to laugh and call him names;
They never let poor Rudolph
Join in any reindeer games.

Then one foggy Christmas Eve,
Santa came to say,
Rudolph with your nose so bright,
Won't you guide my sleigh tonight?

Then how the reindeer loved him
As they shouted out with glee,
Rudolph the Red-Nosed Reindeer,
You'll go down in history.

You know Dasher and Dancer and Prancer and Vixen,
Comet and Cupid and Donner and Blitzen,
But do you recall?
The most famous reindeer of all?

Rudolph the Red-Nosed Reindeer
Had a very shiny nose,
And if you ever saw it,
You would even say it glows. Like a light bulb!
All of the other reindeer
Used to laugh and call him names;
They never let poor Rudolph
Join in any reindeer games.

Then one foggy Christmas Eve,
Santa came to say,
Rudolph with your nose so bright,
Won't you guide my sleigh tonight?
Then how the reindeer loved him
As they shouted out with glee,
Rudolph the Red-Nosed Reindeer,
You'll go down in history.

CHAPTER 11

The Role of 'Noticing' in Learning Grammar

VIJAYA JOHN KOHLI

ABSTRACT

Every language teacher will readily admit that the ability to control grammatical structures is central to linguistic proficiency and that the transmission of the rules of grammar must be an integral part of teaching a language. However, opinion is widely divided over what exactly it means to transmit the rules of grammar effectively: should teachers choose an inductive or a deductive approach? Does an explicit focus on grammatical rules help in any way, or are we better off just doing an interesting 'communicative' task in the classroom?

In this paper, based largely on research in second language acquisition, I shall be arguing that internalised grammatical knowledge can be either declarative or procedural in nature and that there is sufficient evidence to conclude that both these types of knowledge are valuable to language learners. The real question is how we can effectively promote these two types of knowledge. In this paper, I shall suggest some answers to this question, and I shall deal, in particular, with how procedural knowledge can be developed through form-focused classroom tasks which encourage students to 'notice' the rules of grammar.

'KNOWING GRAMMAR' — WHAT DOES IT MEAN?

Learning a language necessarily involves learning its grammar, by which we mean learning to use the right forms of words in sentences and learning the rules relating to the order in which words can occur. Because we have learnt the grammar of English we can, for example, designate as grammatically incorrect such utterances as '*a he saw film Bollywood last the night' and '*He seen a Bollywood film last night'; in contrast, we would accept as perfectly grammatical the sentence, 'He saw a Bollywood film last night'. We can make such grammatical judgements even about sentences we may not quite understand such as, 'He gave her a fongmonistong for her siltering.'

Knowing a language is, of course much more than knowing its grammar, but to the extent that grammar is an integral part of a language, no language can be said to have been learnt or acquired without our having learnt or acquired its grammar. Indeed we can confidently assert that anyone who knows a language knows the rules of the grammar of that language. It is equally clear that a proficient user of two or three languages knows two or three grammars. Yet, the strange thing is that if a proficient user of, say, Hindi is asked if she 'knows Hindi grammar', she is most likely to tell us that she does not know any grammar at all. Why is this the case? Why does a person who knows the grammar of a language well enough to use the language proficiently claim not to know its grammar?

There are two possible explanations for this answer. In the first place, the proficient user may simply be unaware that the sentences she produces so fluently come from a very complex system that exists in her brain, just as someone who can walk with ease may be unaware of the fact that he is relying on a complex anatomical motor system that involves the coordination of several muscles to provide progression while maintaining balance. Likewise, because speaking and walking come so naturally to us as humans, it may well be that many people are unaware of the complexities of the systems that make such abilities possible in the first place. It is only when our skills in walking and talking are underdeveloped or have a break-down that we become aware of the complexity of the systems that make these activities possible.

The second explanation for why a proficient user may deny knowing grammar has to do with our popular understanding of the term 'grammar'. It is commonly assumed that 'knowing grammar' means being able to explain the rules of grammar on the basis of exercises that may have been done at school with terms such as 'noun', 'verb', 'phrase' or 'clause'. In this sense, 'knowing grammar' is regarded as knowledge that has been consciously gained *about* the system of grammatical rules rather than subconsciously gained knowledge *of* the system. The common misconception is that 'knowing grammar' means being able to describe the grammatical rules of a language.

This misunderstanding about what 'knowing grammar' means makes it clear that we need to distinguish between subconsciously gained (or IMPLICIT) grammatical rules which enable us to produce sentences effortlessly, and consciously gained (or EXPLICIT and METALINGUISTIC) rules about grammar which enable us to discuss rule systems and apply them to sample sentences. The first of these types of knowledge, the knowledge that enables us to effortlessly produce appropriate sentences in appropriate contexts, is generally referred to as being an outcome of PROCEDURAL MEMORY. The second type of knowledge, the knowledge that is acquired through conscious and targeted learning, is the outcome of DECLARATIVE MEMORY.

Procedural learning involves learning from experience, involves all the senses and is episodic; declarative learning is cognitive, rational and self-conscious. The difference between the two types of learning is similar to the difference between learning about Delhi through the experience of living in it (procedural) and learning about it, say from a Wikipedia entry (declarative). We see this again as the difference between being a good swimmer on the one hand, and on the other, knowing the theory about what strokes one needs to make in order to swim well.

Research on the human brain includes considerable evidence that procedural and declarative memories are stored in different parts of the brain and function in quite different ways. This fact is highly significant for language teachers and it is therefore worth considering what the differences may be between declarative and procedural learning. In an article entitled 'Neurolinguistics of bilingualism and the teaching of languages', Paradis (2002) draws extensively from studies in the neurosciences and summarises some of the implications of these discoveries for second language learning. Among the points he makes are:

1. That the two types of knowledge, i.e. declarative and procedural, are quite distinct from one another. They '....are of a different nature, bear on different objects, and rely on very different cerebral structures, and that, therefore, metalinguistic knowledge [i.e. declarative knowledge] never becomes implicit competence [i.e. procedural knowledge], or the other way around. Both develop independently.'
2. That the method by which grammar is learnt/ acquired (and by implication, the method by which it is taught) will determine which type of knowledge is being constructed in the learner's brain. Paradis writes:

   > 'To the extent that a language is acquired incidentally, it will be represented as automatically usable implicit competence (and the more so, the younger the individual); to the extent that it is learned formally, it will be represented as metalinguistic knowledge usable in a controlled manner (and the more so, the older the individual). Therefore, the more formal the learning method, the more the second language will rely on declarative memory; the more communicative the method, the more the second language will rely on procedural memory.'

   In other words, a communicative approach will assist procedural learning and a grammar-translation approach, based on doing grammar exercises, will build up declarative learning.
3. That both these types of learning are useful, and can support one another regardless of the fact that they are largely independent systems of learning. We see this, for instance, when people who suffer from brain damage that affects procedural memory can still rely on declarative learning to enable them to communicate. Likewise, those who have suffered loss of declarative memory can still rely on their procedural learning.

This brief overview of the two quite distinct types of learning helps us to understand more precisely what 'knowing grammar' means and how our grammar teaching goals ought to be framed. Since both procedural and declarative learning are useful, although in different ways, I shall assume that it is self-evident that our teaching goals should include the promotion of both types of knowledge.

Declarative Knowledge of Grammar—What Teachers Can Do

The decisions a teacher must make to promote declarative grammatical knowledge are no different from the decisions that will have to be made for the declarative learning of geography or history or economics. Good textbooks that provide an accurate and comprehensive overview of English grammar should be selected, as also grammar exercises meant to provide practice through rule-application. As with syllabi for geography or history, there is much to be said for beginning with relatively simple concepts of grammatical organisation and moving on to increasingly more difficult ones.

Procedural Knowledge of Grammar—How it is Constructed

It has been well-documented in second-language acquisition (SLA) studies that the construction of procedural linguistic knowledge follows quite a different route. A readable overview of these processes can be found in chapter 4 of *How Languages are Learned* by Lightbown & Spada (2006).

The construction of a system of grammar in procedural memory is largely subconscious. It is widely accepted that the learner is subconsciously in the process of trying to make sense of the meaning and the form the language she receives as 'input'. Over a period of time and with increased exposure to language that serves as input, a learner begins to be able to guess what utterances might mean: further exposure to such input will indicate to the learner's subconscious mind whether the initial guesses were correct or wrong. This process of making sense, by guessing, and either confirming or rejecting guesses, is referred to as 'hypothesis formation' and 'hypothesis testing' in SLA studies.

In the early stages of learning, a learner's hypotheses are generally about global meaning and about the organisation of larger units of grammar; over time, these subconscious hypotheses become increasingly more concerned with grammatical details that signify finer distinctions in structure and meaning. Interestingly, the sequences of hypotheses that learners make are predictable. Various types of work in SLA (see Pienemann 1998) suggest that there are clearly characterisable, stages and routes through which every learner must go in learning a language. Just as it is normal for babies to learn to crawl before they can walk, and both the crawling and the walking reflect different stages in the baby's state of development as an organism, so also there are stages in the learning of grammar which reflect developments in the learner's capacity to process language.

Our discussion thus far has focussed on how procedural knowledge of grammar is constructed; I have emphasised the role of the learner's sub-conscious system in formulating and testing hypotheses and the role of the input which the learner receives as providing the language material that generates and corrects hypotheses. The question that we must now ask is how this information can be used by teachers to promote procedural learning in their students.

Procedural Learning—What Teachers Can Do

While the teacher has the controlling hand in promoting declarative learning, the promotion of procedural learning cannot be thus controlled: it can only be facilitated. It is therefore important for the teacher to understand what she can do in order to facilitate procedural learning in the classroom.

Input

Since procedural learning takes place through the formation and testing of hypotheses about the structure of language, the teacher must ensure that learners engage with sufficiently rich and sufficiently abundant instances of language. Unfortunately, the input provided in most classrooms may simply not be complex enough or sufficiently standard for the development of accuracy and proficiency.

Therefore, teachers must place a very high premium on an abundance of reading and listening activities which engage many aspects of a learner's imagination. Stories at the early stages and full-length novels at the intermediate and advanced stages are highly recommended. For schools that do not have library resources at hand, I strongly recommend the freely downloadable collection of books from Project Gutenberg. Similarly, listening to recorded stories at an early stage, and audio-novels and long lectures at the intermediate and advanced stages is highly recommended. There is a wealth of excellent audio material on the net that teachers and students can use: BBC news broadcasts, the hundreds of programmes listed on BBC 4 internet radio and on Librivox, TED talks, and the BBC Reith lectures are just a few of the enormous store of good audio resources that are freely available on the net.

Learning Activities and Tasks

Asking students to read or listen more, however, is unlikely to be sufficient; it is a part of the teacher's responsibilities to create purpose-driven tasks for reading and listening activities. Such tasks may take a variety of forms. Students could be asked, for instance, to make a time-lime for the plot of a story that has been read, or heard; or, they might be asked to make suggestions about how they would adapt certain parts of the story into a Bollywood script; or, they could be asked to convert it into a graphic narrative, or a dramatic script. The possibilities are numerous; for those who run out of ideas, there are many suggestions that can be followed in books such as Morgan and Rinvolucri (1983), Day and Bamford (1998) and Wajnryb (2003).

From the learning perspective, what is important in designing such tasks is to ensure that the tasks involve input that is varied and complex in quality and abundant in quantity.

Grammatical Accuracy in Procedural Memory: 'Noticing'

Providing good input through engaging tasks meets an essential condition for language learning as a whole, but it does not necessarily hasten the process of fostering grammatical accuracy. And, as we have already seen, grammar taught explicitly becomes a part of declarative knowledge and does not necessarily become a part of procedural memory. So, the problem that now confronts us is how we can promote what Larsen-Freeman (2003) has referred to as 'grammaring', that is, how we can promote grammatical accuracy implicitly and as a part of procedural learning.

It is widely believed that activities that promote the 'noticing' of grammatical details help learners to make the right types of choices during the subconscious process of forming and testing hypotheses about grammar. 'Noticing', as the term is generally used in applied linguistics, refers to the process in which the learner pays particular attention to a specific aspect of grammar which eventually goes on to become a part of her implicit learning. Noticing helps learners to make hypotheses that reflect the rules of standard English grammar; failure to notice, on the other hand, can lead learners to repeatedly make grammatical mistakes in certain areas.

The implication for teachers is clear: in addition to communicative tasks based on varied and abundant input, we also need to have tasks and activities that promote procedural learning ('grammaring') through 'noticing'. In other words, we need what Long (1991) has referred to as tasks that 'focus on FORM'. According to Long, 'Focus on Form' tasks contrast with both tasks that 'focus on meaning', which engage procedural memory, and on 'focus on FORM**S**' activities which are based on explicit grammar-teaching and engage declarative memory.

The points I have made thus far can be represented as given below:

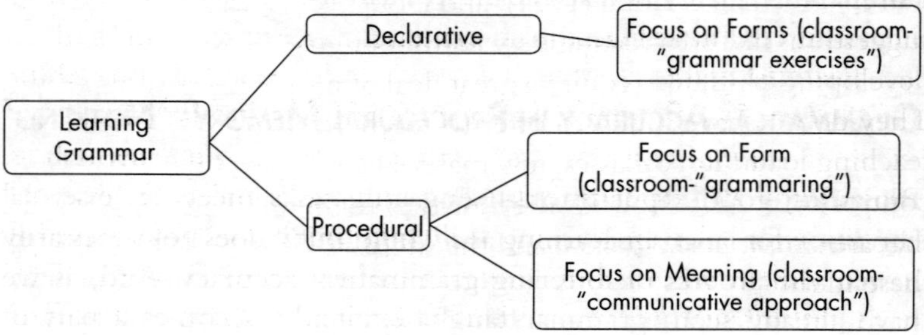

It needs to be emphasised here that communicative, meaning-based activities are just not sufficient for the promotion of grammatical accuracy. Grammatical organisation has a great deal of redundancy and an emphasis on recognising meaning does not mean that the complexities of grammatical organisation have also been recognised.

Let us illustrate this with an example. Consider the following sentence:

These dogs are hungry.

The idea that this refers to *more than one* canine creature is marked *three times* in the grammar (*these, dogs, are*) Yet, it has been shown, time and again, that many learners pick up only the most obvious marker, the plural *-s* in *dogs*, and ignore the other markers altogether. Thus the learner may have got the right meaning (of plurality), but when required to produce similar sentences will produce structures such as.*This dogs is hungry* or **These dogs is hungry* or **This dogs are hungry*. The emphasis on meaning alone is clearly insufficient for the learning of grammar.

In the next section, I shall look briefly at a few activities that teachers can use in classrooms to get their students to focus on grammatical form; such (subconscious) attention paid to form will promote proficiency.

Activities that Promote Noticing

Activities to promote noticing have been suggested by a number of specialists such as Sharwood Smith (1981) and (1994); Ellis (2003); Larsen-Freeman & Long (1991); and Doughty (1991). Some of these suggestions involve creating new textbooks with different layouts, or developing tasks that require a great deal of ingenuity from teachers. They do not have much to offer to teachers who might have high teaching loads, large classes, few material resources and very limited control over the textbooks they have to use in class. We need tasks that are simple and effective and the suggestions given below reflect these ideals.

Dictation Activities

Dictation, which used to be a common classroom activity, has been dropped in many classrooms; if it is used at all, it is seen primarily as a means of checking if students can spell correctly. This is unfortunate as dictation, in several variations, can help students to focus on different types of language data, including grammatical structure.

(i) *Grammar dictation or dictagloss*

One of the most widely used activities for grammar teaching is 'Grammar Dictation' or 'Dictagloss'. Here the teacher reads aloud, twice and at normal speed, a short text (4–6 sentences) which contains examples of the grammar that the teacher wants students to notice. Students are then asked to reconstruct, in pairs, or groups of four, every word of the text that was read out aloud. Students usually find the task very frustrating because they haven't been able to write down much of what was read; their grammatical confusions surface when they interact in groups, and they try to fill in all the missing bits in their texts. In my classes, when the time for group-work has run out, I usually ask one group to write its answer on the board while the other groups are allowed to suggest alternatives. My own answer comes in the end.

This exercise puts students in a situation where they have to explicitly discuss internalised grammatical rules. There are a number of good texts for this task in Wajnryb (1990); some ELT websites also offer texts that can be used. The exercise can be adapted to all levels of learners.

(ii) *Wall-dictation*

The procedure for this variation of dictation is simple: students working in pairs dictate a text to each other; however, the text to be dictated is not given to them, but is stuck on the walls of the classroom. One student from each pair goes to the wall where the text is located, silently reads what has been written, and then returns to dictate the text to the partner. When half the text has been so dictated, the scribe and the carrier change places.

In my classes I normally choose a short story as the text and I cut it up into 10–14 parts. Each part is given a letter (A to M, for example), and stuck up on different walls in the classroom. The students are asked to form pairs, and the pairs are also assigned alphabets: the idea is that pair A uses text A, and so on. The students are then asked to reconstruct their respective texts through the carrier-scribe interaction. When they have finished, each pair can go to the wall and correct their own mistakes. When everyone is done, the whole class forms a circle and each pair reads out its part of the story for the benefit of the others, till the whole class has read/heard the story.

Texts that I have used with a great deal of success are Oscar Wilde's 'The Model Millionaire', 'Lamb to the Slaughter', by Roald Dahl and O. Henry's 'The Gift of the Magi'. This exercise too can be adapted to learners of all levels.

(iii) *Transcribing tasks—BBC internet news broadcasts*

Getting students to regularly transcribe spoken language texts as a part of their homework is one of the most useful noticing activities I have ever used. Among upper-intermediate students, for instance, I routinely expect students to transcribe at least two full BBC internet news broadcasts of five minutes each over a period of a month. The rules are very simple: students download the broadcast, and can listen to it any number of times, but they must achieve the highest possible accuracy in recording what was said before they submit their transcript. Any words that they are unfamiliar with must be researched and learnt. I usually get students to keep a record of how much time they took to transcribe one minute of audio text. In the beginning, poor students are likely to need several repetitions of text, and are likely to take a very long time to transcribe even a few sentences. Over a period of time, say two weeks, they are likely to have become far quicker and far more accurate. This can be interpreted as arising from a greater degree of inward (procedural) familiarity with the grammatical structures of language.

It must be added that the BBC internet news is especially suited for this exercise since these broadcasts typically involve long grammatical structures with multiple clauses, meaning references that include a range of time and space locations, and from the phonological aspect, a good sample of a varieties of accents.

(iv) *Self-generated transcribing tasks*

For highly-motivated students at lower levels of proficiency, who are weak in all skills, and for those who lack access to the BBC internet archives, even more simple, self-generated transcription tasks are possible. In such cases, students should read aloud and record a chapter they have not understood well. The recording should be reasonably long, say, at least two pages of text. The student must then put away the source book, and attempt to transcribe from the audio text that s/he has created. Here again, the emphasis should be on 100% accuracy. In the final stage, the written version can be compared with the printed version.

This exercise is simple but it promotes noticing at four different stages: at the reading stage, at the listening stage, at the writing stage and finally at the comparing stage. Regular practice in this exercise will help students to acquire grammatical proficiency provided that the texts they choose are in standard English and are not always too simple.

Shadowing or Repetition Activities

Structuralist drills often require students to repeat sentences said by an instructor and it has been shown that this approach has limited value. However, repetition as a strategy has possibilities for the promotion of noticing if it is of naturally occurring speech or authentic texts. To repeat exactly what someone has just said is to 'shadow' their speech; shadowing necessarily implies close attention to details of speech.

It is easy in classrooms for teachers to make up shadowing games, as, say, where one student provides two sentences of a story and the next student has to shadow those sentences and provide two more of her own, and so on. However, such games may not be useful unless the teacher corrects mistakes in the sentences formulated by each student and the corrected versions are shadowed.

Among students who are willing to go the extra mile to improve their own learning I normally recommend 'mental speech shadowing' of BBC internet news broadcasts or the Reith Lectures. Any freely available recorded lecture /short story in Standard English can provide the basis for mental shadowing where the learner repeats in his/her mind what s/he has just heard. Ideally, the learner should listen to the audio-text at least twice: the first time to make sense of what was said and the second to simply shadow the exact words that were used.

Conclusion

The aim of this contribution has been to suggest that the development of grammatical accuracy in procedural memory is implicit and structured in complicated ways. For teachers this means that we do not (yet) know whether grammatical accuracy can be taught for procedural learning; however, we do know that it can be learnt, and we do know that one prerequisite is 'noticing' grammar. As resourceful teachers we can ensure that some of our classroom activities are regularly dedicated to activities that foster the implicit development of grammar.

References

Day, R. R. & J. Bamford, (1998). *Extensive Reading in the Second Language Classroom*. Cambridge: Cambridge University Press.

Doughty, C., (2003). 'Instructed SLA: Constraints, compensation, and enhancement'. In C. Doughty & M. H. Long (eds), *Handbook of Second Language Acquisition*. New York: Blackwell, 256–310.

Ellis, R., (1997). *SLA Research and Language Teaching*. Oxford: Oxford University Press.

——— (2003) *Task-based Language Learning and Teaching*. Oxford: Oxford University Press

Fotos, S., (1993). 'Consciousness-raising and noticing through focus on form: Grammar task performance versus formal instruction'. *Applied Linguistics*, 14/4, 385–407.

Larsen-Freeman, D., (2003). *Teaching Language: From Grammar to Grammaring*. Boston: Thomson-Heinle.

Larsen-Freeman, D. & M. Long, (1991). *An Introduction to Second Language Acquisition Research*. London: Longman.

Lightbown, P. & N. M. Spada, (2006). *How Languages Are Learned*. Oxford: Oxford University Press.

Long, M., (1991). 'Focus on form: A design feature in language teaching methodology'. In K. de Bot, R. Ginsberg, & C. Kramsch (eds), *Foreign Language Research in Cross-cultural Perspective*. Amsterdam: John Benjamins, 39–52.

Long, M. H. & G. Crookes, (1992). 'Three approaches to task-based language teaching'. *TESOL Quarterly*, 26/1, 27–56.

Morgan, J. & M. Rinvolucri, (1983). *Once Upon a Time: Using Stories in the Language Classroom*. Cambridge: Cambridge

Paradis, M., (2002). 'Neurolinguistics of bilingualism and the teaching of languages'. *Symposium On the Multimodality of Human Communication: Theories, Problems and Applications*, University of Toronto. Published in *Semioticon*. URL: http://www. semioticon.com/virtuals/talks/paradis. pdf. Last accessed on 18 November 2016.

——— (1994). 'Neurolinguistic aspects of implicit and explicit memory: Implications for bilingualism and SLA'. In N. Ellis (ed.), *Implicit and Explicit Learning of Languages*. New York: Academic Press, 393–420.

Pienemann, M., (1998). *Language Processing and Second Language Development: Processability Theory (Studies in Bilingualism, 15)*. Amsterdam, Philadelphia: John Benjamins Publishing Company.

Smith, M. Sharwood, (1994). *Second Language Learning: Theoretical Foundations*. London: Longman.

——— (1981) 'Consciousness-raising and the second language learner'. *Applied Linguistics, 2/2, 159–68.*

Wajnryb, R., (1990). *Grammar Dictation*. Oxford: Oxford University Press.

——— (2003) *Stories: Narrative Activities for the Language Classroom*. Cambridge: Cambridge

CHAPTER 12

Exploring Multiple Intelligences through Storytelling in the Classroom

SHEFALI RAY

ABSTRACT

Storytelling is a powerful tool in the classroom, especially with young learners, who emote with it, respond to it intellectually, constructing in their own individual ways the meaning of what they encounter in the tale or the telling. A story can be exploited in multiple ways that may range from language development, knowledge gain, or new insights, to the instilling and invigorating of personal or social values and creativity. At times it provides a sense of catharsis, as well.

Emotional intelligence and multiple intelligences can be stimulated in the process of storytelling. Application of the Multiple Intelligences Theory allows us to tap into the whole language skills, learning processes, social dynamics and learning strategies. Since it recognises the diversity amongst students, a teacher finds the situation of storytelling to be a comfortable fit, since the possibilities of exploring the intelligences are immense. A teacher may organise a range of activities depending upon the intelligences she wishes to explore, hone or exercise. These may include problem-solving, summarising, evaluating, dramatisation, visualisation, socialisation or personalisation, to mention a few. Activities can be organised focusing on certain specific intelligences during different stages of storytelling which generally begin with receiving and responding to the story and proceed on to a creative retelling and extension of it. This would allow learners with varying dominant intelligences to feel comfortable to a certain degree and enable them to contribute actively to the learning experience thus reinforcing their own self-worth as well. Learners can enrich a learning situation by bringing to it their life experiences and background knowledge, their ideas, perceptions, presentations, creativity and language skills.

INTRODUCTION

Storytelling has been a medium of transmitting knowledge and culture and a tool for rekindling community memory. It remains a potent tool in the classroom even today and greatly so with young learners, who emote with the character and the situation. During various sessions of storytelling, with different target groups, it was found that stories have an appeal to all age groups, provided listeners get an opportunity to seek analogies with what they have learnt and experienced during the telling and after. In other words, it allows them to explore their own world with a new perspective. Thus, stories that are rooted in reality in one way or the other or are an imaginative presentation of reality, work well with them.

Storytelling is a potent tool for it lends to language development, appreciation of literature, development of critical thinking skills and critical comprehension, an understanding of community and self, development of empathy and creativity. In addition, storytelling has been found to yield a heightened sense of social cohesiveness amongst listeners and activate the contribution of individual ideas and talent to a common pool during collaborative activities.

Storytelling as a Potential Tool to Exercise Multiple Intelligences

Multiple intelligences can be exercised through discussions, drawing and painting activities, group activities like miming and dramatising, recreating and extending and personalising during a storytelling session.

The theory of multiple intelligences (MI) was propounded by Howard Gardner in 1983 wherein he stated that it is possible for an individual to excel in different fields, not necessarily the logical and mathematical one, the then existing yardstick of intelligence. To mention briefly, the intelligences identified by him were, bodily-kinaesthetic (learn better by muscular movement), logical-mathematical (problem-solving), verbal-linguistic (working with language), interpersonal (to do with human relationships and a sensitivity to other people's moods, emotions and needs), intrapersonal (introspective and self-reflective), visual-spatial (spatial management, visualisation and being artistically inclined), musical (greater sensitivity to rhythm, sounds and tones) and naturalistic (showing greater awareness of nature and sensitivity towards it).

The multiple intelligence theory has led to the tapping of whole language skills in learning situations, processes and strategies. It recognises the diversity amongst students and emphasises the use of interpersonal, creative, communicative and interactive skills in a learning situation. An intuitive teacher recognises the need to exercise various intelligences and designs a variety of activities that provide individuals with an opportunity to exercise their dominant intelligences, and do what they can do best, while allowing others to exercise the same in order to develop or hone them. The paper will explore some of the ways MI's can be exploited or exercised through storytelling.

The Role of Emotional Intelligence in the Delivery and Reception of a Story

On the other hand, emotional intelligence, conceptualised by Goleman in 1995, emphasised the importance of the emotions in our cognitive processing. According to him, persons who manage their emotions tend to be more capable of fully intelligent processing. And storytelling allows the listeners to explore and express their own emotions when they respond to the situations in the story as they identify with the protagonist, partaking of the emotional situation and using their schema to interpret, analogise and conclude.

Individual listeners construct meaning or arrive at interpretations unique to themselves in which their individual schema and personality factors contribute vitally. Post-listening discussions thus yield a great diversity in the ways actions and motives of characters are interpreted. Multiple intelligences can be exercised through discussions, drawing and painting activities, group activities like miming and dramatising, recreating and extending the story and personalising it.

Storytelling with Young Learners

During numerous storytelling sessions, both within the classroom and in open storytelling sessions with the young, mainly two stories were used. The target group of the sessions held in the primary classes had a fairly good competence in the use of English, being held in private schools. The target group of the open sessions had mixed ability children within ages ranging from twelve to six. So basically, their comprehension of the language was good.

One of the stories used was 'The Song of the Scarecrow', by Suddhasattwa Basu in which a scarecrow, wishing to see new places and have some fun, leaves its post and wanders about playfully singing a song. On his return, he is shocked to find his field ravaged by marauding birds. The glee is immediately replaced by regret and remorse. He realises that everyone has a role to play and dereliction of duty can lead to pain and loss.

The other story was 'The Princess with the Longest Hair' by Komilla Raote, is about a princess with very long hair that continues to grow. It is cared for and nurtured by her many servants. She lives in the lap of luxury but is restricted to her room, being unable to walk because of the weight of her hair. On her birthday, which also marks the day her hair would reach the ground when let out of a window of the topmost room in the palace, she decides to abandon her father's house and the grand celebration planned for the occasion. She pulls off her tresses and donates them to help humans and animals alike, till there is no hair left on her head. And that is a happy moment for her. She skips and sings and walks to the other side of the hill never to be seen again. The hill, bare for so long, suddenly blooms with plants and animal life.

The Telling of the Story

As the story was narrated, different responses were received, that varied from the simple acceptance and immersion in the storyline, to a skeptical questioning of motives and actions. Some listeners were emotionally moved in a direct bonding with the protagonist and some took the story with a pinch of salt.

In brief, these were the various responses received during the telling:

- getting immersed in the story and not interrupting the telling
- receiving the story in an animated and emotional manner, emoting with the characters, their emotions being directly reflected on their faces
- being skeptical and asking questions discounting the possibility of something happening like a scarecrow coming to life, or a girl pulling off her own hair (logical-mathematical)
- directly bonding with the protagonist (sometimes with an expression of pain or tears)
- visualising the scene in their mind's eye (visual and spatial) and describing it

Post-Listening Activities

Responding to the story

During the post-telling session, the young learners or children again responded to the stories in various ways. Most of the learners said that they liked the story but there were stray instances where some raised serious objections to certain aspects of the story. By and large, the unreal and the fantasy element had an appeal for them.

Some of the responses to the questions and ideas expressed in the ensuing discussion, demonstrative of linguistic intelligence, are listed:

- a clear demarcation between the right and wrong actions since neither of the stories had any antagonists (remotely the birds in the field)
- empathy for the protagonist (the princess) feeling that she was sad as she was denied a childhood

- a strong sense of appreciation for what the princess had done, her kindness towards those she met
- a judgmental attitude towards the actions of the scarecrow, who they felt was neglecting his duty (logical-mathematical, interpersonal)
- one or two stray instances of rejection of the parents of the princess, for denying her the right to go to school or have friends or play with (interpersonal)
- mention of some of the new things learnt during the listening of the story (tacit knowledge, intrapersonal)
- personalising the story by saying what they would have done in the place of the protagonists (intrapersonal)
- mentioning what they liked or did not like in the story (intrapersonal)

Recreating the story

Though the children enjoyed the animated discussion, they liked recreating the story through kinaesthetic activities more. They enjoyed role play and mime, illustrated with brief dialogues. Some of the other activities that exercised the linguistic, spatial, interpersonal, intrapersonal and logical-mathematical intelligences were:

- miming scenes from the story for others to guess and narrate the event, like the stance of the scarecrow, his walk and his expression of shock; the laboured gait of the princess because of her long hair and her skipping gait after she has lost all her hair (kinaesthetic)
- dramatising scenes especially the ones which required large participation like the train of servants holding the hair of the princess as she walked, the marauding birds, the coming to life of the scarecrow and the leaps and skips he makes on his sojourn; the princess gifting her hair to the needy etc. (interpersonal, linguistic and kinaesthetic)
- imagining and drawing the picture of the princess or the scarecrow (spatial)

- painting a terracotta pot to make the face of the scarecrow and putting straw as hair and a paper hat (this was the most popular post-listening activity)
- physically demonstrating the happy scarecrow and the sad and chastised scarecrow and similarly the sad and uncomfortable princess and the happy princess with no hair on her head (kinaesthetic)
- singing the song of the scarecrow (musical)

Extending the story

When asked how they would like the story to continue, some of the responses were the conventional ones, while there were a few children who chose to be radically different. Their responses clearly indicated the use of the logical-mathematical intelligence and a lot of language. These included:

- the scarecrow has learnt a lesson that he has a responsibility and promises to be a good boy henceforth (linguistic, intrapersonal and logical mathematical)
- the scarecrow has discovered the pleasures of wandering and decides to take a trip again (linguistic and intrapersonal)
- the farmer comes and replaces the scarecrow with a more frightening looking one (linguistic and logical-mathematical)
- the princess is happy as she has gone to another kingdom and promises never to return to her father's kingdom (linguistic, interpersonal and intrapersonal)
- she has gone to heaven and that is how the people can still hear her song when there is a strong wind (linguistic)
- her father regrets not understanding her emotional and social needs and repents his actions (linguistic, intrapersonal, logical-mathematical)

It was noticed that learners thus constructed meaning using their individual cognitive resources. They accumulated tacit knowledge from the presentation of unfamiliar situations as many city children had not seen a scarecrow. They interpreted actions and motives in their own ways. They made their own predictions and anticipated what is to come next in the telling. They learnt about cause and effect (dereliction of duty and result), logical sequences, human relationships (parent's ambition and demands on the child), motives and actions (the running away of the princess, the innocent wandering of the scarecrow) with an overriding sense of right or wrong, or of behavioural excesses on the part of a character (scarecrow's leaving his post and the father's virtual imprisonment of his daughter caused by her very long hair) by cultural or modern norms (rights of the child). They also learnt to contribute to the creation of something new by participating in group activities that focus on retelling and extending the story.

Some of the Gains of the Storytelling Session

The gains mentioned below are not restricted merely to these two stories but those discerned over multiple storytelling session with different target groups using diverse stories.

The gains that were noticed during storytelling sessions were:

- a settling effect on the young children, who otherwise have a short attention span
- development of critical thinking by not accepting things at their face value
- heightened social cohesiveness and collaboration through group activities
- heightened feeling of empathy
- transfer of knowledge gained or experiences to the storytelling sessions (recent learning of child's rights applied to the situation of the princess and conclusions drawn)
- heightened creativity
- development of language skills (new vocabulary, expressions or social formulae)
- active contribution to the activity as per one's ability (oral communication, drawing and painting, miming and dramatising, critically examining characters, actions and situations)

Storytelling to Teenagers

Several stories have been used with teenagers, mainly from the government schools under the access programme of the American Centre and trainee teachers during storytelling demonstrations. These range from the classics to the modern by western and Indian authors, over a period of five years.

The themes, genres and cultures of the stories being varied that lent to a range of activities, 'A Sound Payment' will be considered for the purpose of this essay.

A Sound Payment (A broad outline)
By Shefali Ray

A poor man, Abdullah, is out of work. For lack of anything better to do, he strolls in the marketplace in the evening. Starving due to lack of food, he is attracted to a small eating place but has no money to buy any. So he decides to play a guessing game based on the flavours that rise from the dishes that are served in a small eating house. He smells deeply muttering to himself the name of each dish. This does not seem to help much as he gets hungrier. As he is about to move away from the shop he is accosted by the owner who demands the price of the smell of all the food he has inhaled so eagerly and deeply. Abdullah tries to reason with the owner but he would have nothing of it and drags him to the Qazi's court. It being evening, the court is closing and Abdullah is asked to appear in court the next day for the hearing. Frightened that he may be punished, he seeks Mullah Nasruddin's help and tells him his sad story. The following day Nasruddin accompanies him to court and allows the case to drift in favour of the shop owner. When the time for payment comes, he requests the Qazi to allow him to pay on behalf of Abdullah. That is gladly agreed upon. He moves close to the man and shakes a cloth bag full of coins. The coins jingle loudly and he asks the man if he can hear the money. Anticipating payment the man nods in the affirmative and Nasruddin tells him that he has been paid and rightly so, since Abdullah had smelt his food and he has heard the jingle of his money. Neither the man nor the Qazi have anything more to say. Abdullah escapes the punishment he would have got for no fault of his.

(Adapted from 'A Sound Payment' by Shefali Ray, *Reading with Joy II*, SCERT, Delhi, 1999)

The Telling of the Story

Since the target group comprised senior school students and trainee teachers for a live demonstration of a storytelling session in school, the story was narrated without any interruption as the students took the events of the story in their stride accepting it as simply an interesting story. Some were familiar with the character of Mullah Nasruddin and half expected 'the twist in the tail' kind of end to the story.

The telling was largely uneventful with no questions asked but ended with laughter at the intelligent strategy of the Mullah, a clear indication that they felt a sense of relief at the reprieve of the protagonist. It would be worth mentioning here that the trainees were not very competent in English themselves.

Post-Listening Activities

Receiving and responding to the story

The post-listening questions, both of the recollect kind and the inferential kind led to an animated discussion. The listeners felt that motives of both Abdullah and the eating-house owner could be questioned. A few felt that Abdullah was not right in standing and sniffing at the food being served, or was naïve enough to think that his act would not be objected to. All, however, empathised with him and felt that he was wronged (interpersonal). The motives and attitudes attributed to the actions and words of the characters were the following:

- naïve attitude of Abdullah to think that he could sniff at the food in a food stall and not be reprimanded for it

- the greed of the eating-shop owner who was on the lookout for a quick buck
- the attitude of the have's towards the have-not's, a general intolerance and punishing attitude
- the attitude of the Qazi who was openly in favour of the unrealistic demand of the eating-shop owner
- the smartness and the mental agility of the Mullah who showed the eating-shop owner and the Qazi how unreasonable they had been

Some of the students even felt that the Mullah ought to have asked the eating-house owner for compensation for harassing a poor man. The discussion clearly reflected the students' experiences and knowledge of the society in which they lived with all its failings and weaknesses.

Recreating the story

Both school and college students showed great involvement in the successive activities, ranging from the visual, spatial, inter and intrapersonal to linguistic and kinaesthetic. It was observed that the school students remained true to the story while recreating it in the form of a pageant or a freeze frame while the college students added bits of their own to make the scenes more alive or to incorporate all group members in the scene. There were innovations made by both kinds of students.

Some of the activities that explored many of the intelligences, especially the linguistic and logical-mathematical ones, were the most successful:

- recreating the scenes using dialogues (linguistic, interpersonal, logical-mathematical)
- miming and freeze-frame involving participation of every member of the group by representing even non-living things like the Qazi's table or the door or even flapping curtains (spatial, linguistic, interpersonal)
- adding new characters while rewriting and enacting certain scenes (linguistic, interpersonal, intrapersonal)

- creating dialogues using the day-to-day language, often adding formulaic expressions (linguistic, interpersonal)
- a narrator beginning to tell the story followed by relevant characters stepping in and taking over, narrating what happened to them at that point in the story (linguistic, interpersonal, intrapersonal)
- narrator telling the story as the characters mime the scene (linguistic and kinaesthetic)
- preparing line drawings depicting their favourite scenes from the story and retelling the story using the drawings as clues (intrapersonal, spatial and linguistic)
- playing the game 'hot seat' with different characters of the story, exploring intentions, motives and values (interpersonal, intrapersonal and linguistic)
- creating interesting dialogues using day to day language and often lapsing into Hindi (linguistic)

Extending or rewriting the story

The activities involved going beyond the story and telling how it would have proceeded from where it ended last. The rewriting activities were based on the new problem that the protagonist Abdullah is supposed to face—his inability to meet the Mullah before the judgement. Students had to think of other plausible ways in which Abdullah received help. This activity yielded delightful results with the college going students, adding characters and new events. They were required to create the situation, work on the dialogues, allocate roles and enact the scene before the class. This gave an insight into how they perceived right and wrong and thought of ways the right could be helped. Hence, new characters were created many of whom were women and who are instrumental in helping Abdullah.

This demonstrated how a storyteller can help learners to construct meaning in their own way, make interpretations of their own, reconstruct the story in different ways using different media, expand and extend the story in groups. The variety in the activities enabled the learners with different intelligences to put in their best according to the demands of the activity and help the others exercise the same intelligence to hone it. The best part of these activities was the sense of involvement and a feeling of ownership towards what they had created. As is evident from the variety in the activities, multiple intelligences were exercised and honed. As is evident from the activities and the responses different intelligences were exercised in the activities.

To conclude, it can be said that the vibrancy of the post-listening activities does not take away the pure joy of listening, the feeling of wonder that every story offers.

The students mentioned in the paper belong to various government and private schools of Delhi where the investigator conducted storytelling sessions and two colleges of the Delhi University where the investigator was demonstrating storytelling to teacher trainees.

References

Ajex, N. K., (1988). *Storytelling: Its Wide-Ranging Impact in the Classroom.* ERIC Digest no. 9, ERIC Clearninghouse on Reading and Communication Skills. Bloomington, IN.

Basu, S., (2002). *The Song of the Scarecrow*. New Delhi: Katha.

Gardner, H., (1983). *Multiple Intelligences.* New York: Basic Books.

Goleman, D., (1995). *Emotional Intelligence.* New York: Bantam Books.

Raote, K., (1998). *The Princess with the Longest Hair.* New Delhi: Katha.

Ray, S., (1999). *A Sound Payment: Reading with Joy.* New Delhi: SCERT.

Rosen, H., (1986). 'The Importance of Story'. *Language Arts*, 63/3, Pembroke Publishers, 226–37.

CHAPTER 13

Language Teaching in Inclusive Education

SANTOSH KUMAR

Abstract

'The only principle that allows us to evaluate individual behaviour and social situations is the recognition of the political, social, and cultural rights of all human beings, who are viewed as free and equal. The individual must be treated as the cornerstone of a reconstructed sociology' (Alain Touraine 2009 in Thinking Differently).

This paper seeks to draw attention on the expressed line of philosophy, to challenges in language teaching to disabled people in general and children with Learning Disabilities (LD) in particular. The primary purpose of this discussion is to provide a new orientation to applied linguistics to take a step towards inclusive education by drawing insights from Disability Studies (DS) worldwide on one hand, and socially relevant issues in multicultural societies which include disabled people as a community on the other.[1]

Introduction

The essay explores the nature of the contents of language curriculum in the light of disability studies in inclusive education. The nature of content of the language curriculum in inclusive education is considered from the point of view of disabled

[1] I would like to acknowledge my sincere thanks to Professor Rama Kant Agnihotri for encouraging me to write this paper.

students in general, with an exemplar of students with learning disabilities. The exemplar of students with learning disabilities raises the issue of language difference and learning difference in the education of disabled students. There have been studies on this assumption in and outside of linguistics as well. The kind of research on language acquisition, especially on persons with LD, in Psycholinguistics, and Neurolinguistics has been carried out in medical models of disability which locates the 'disability' within the individual and so whatever the level of achievement, it is attributed to individual. There are studies in Clinical Linguistics which has a description of the 'impairment' as one of its aim.

Tom Shakespeare (2007) observes that disability is a complex, scalar, multi-dimensional phenomenon. Disability is considered to be the result of impairment that may be physical, cognitive, sensory, or some combination of all these that turns out to be a hindrance in participating in what is thought to be 'normal' activities in day-to-day life. Learning disabilities are conditions which affect the acquisition, organisation and retention of linguistic skills.

The disability rights movements helped to construct the disabled as a political category to encompass the diverse range of people with impairments, advocating their rights to live life with dignity, free from stereotypes and stigma and as regular or 'normal' people (Mehrotra 2011). The social exclusion and devaluation of disabled people is widespread and persistent. The social model of disability envisages that disability lies in the structure of society rather than in individual. It is the social model of disability which conceptualises and explores the role of barriers and oppression in the lives of disabled people. The United Nations Convention on the Rights of Persons with Disabilities (UNCRPD, 2006) states that 'Persons with disabilities include those who have long-term physical, mental, intellectual or sensory impairments which, in interaction with various *barriers*, may hinder their full and effective participation in society on an equal basis with others' (Article 1, italics mine). The *barrier* is the catch word which ranges from the physical to psychological barriers and restricts the movement of disabled people. Education is one of the spheres where disabled students face barriers of pedagogies in form and contents.

The discussion roots into the philosophical assumption that 'we all are abled or disabled in some or the other way'. It implies that disabled people are so-called 'disabled' in the normative culture, so the normal or abled people of one culture become 'disabled' in another culture. To give an analogy, for example, from the theoretical development on Second Language Acquisition (SLA) in general and English Language Teaching (ELT) for Indian students in particular (Agnihotri & Khanna 1994, 1995; and Agnihotri, Khanna & Sachdev 1998), as most of the papers of the series held in unison that the structures of English language and pedagogical material which is based on English literature pose 'difficulties' or 'impediments' for Indian students and make them 'disabled' to get native-like linguistic fluency, in the same way, pedagogical materials based on the experiences of 'normal' or 'abled-bodied' may pose 'difficulties' for persons with disabilities. It is interesting to note that while the 'difficulties' of normal learners have been perceived by researchers as the 'problem' of pedagogy (Mehrotra 1995; Narula 1995; Vanikar & Palia 1995) and they all suggested a need of such a pedagogical model based in the Indian context so the second language learners can benefit from that. A more vivid example comes from the British approaches to deaf education, the 'old' orders of discourse focused entirely on the promotion of English as the language standard, through the practice of oral/aural, underpinned by the oppressive philosophy of oralism, or phonocentricism (Coker 2000). Psychologists in Britain and the USA identified the poor levels of educational attainment by deaf children, their so called 'linguistic impoverishment' (Conrad 1979) and their 'deficient' psychological and emotional functioning (Levine 1981). Though, this case is dealt in the context of bilingual education and violation of linguistic rights which leads to human rights issue for the deaf community. This gives one the opportunity to ponder upon the importance of the mother tongue in education which is current in multilingual education as well. The issue got resolved in Britain and the USA by the introduction of sign language as medium of instruction in 'bimodal' communication (Corker 1997).

Taking this analogy in account, this essay proposes to restructure language pedagogy according to the needs and experiences of disabled students. To validate the proposition, I will report a study on the acquisition of proverbs in children with LD. Case & Taylor (2005) in their study, 'Language difference or learning disability? Answers from a linguistic perspective', problematise and speculate whether the 'difficulties' in learning proverbs are inherent in disabled children or it is because of *language difference* which they have. Though, the authors do not suggest a definite answer, the question raised the need of more research on the question. The authors held that 'their evaluation for special education services presents significant challenges to ESL, general education, and special education instructors'. However, this is just the 'tip' of a larger question and allows us to look at the various processes involved in language teaching, especially pedagogical material and medium of instruction in the multicultural context.

The motivation for this discussion comes from the statistical data of low literacy rate of disabled people. Literacy and level of education are the basic indicators of the level of development achieved by society. Literacy helps to form the overall development of individuals, enabling them to comprehend their social, political, and cultural environment better and respond to it appropriately. Literacy and education act as a catalyst for social change. The 15th Census of India, 2011 shows the literacy rate in the country as a whole is 74.04%. However, it is estimated that only 49% of the disabled population is literate and only 26% reach the primary school level, 6% complete middle level and only 13% manage to get to the secondary level and above.

There is a marginal increase in the number of disabled people reaching up to secondary level and above when compared to Census 2001. While the literacy levels of the disabled population was only 49 %, the National Sample Survey Organisation (NSSO) 2002 figures show that only 9% got to complete their secondary education and above. The increase in literacy rate at the secondary level in disabled people is just 4%. It is important to explore the reasons behind this low literacy rate and drop-out after middle level education. This low and slow rate is certainly alarming for disability activists and scholars who ask the question whether the government just wants to provide formal education or just literacy skills that will aid the move towards consumerism. The focus on 'social training', 'general life skills' and specialist disability skills work against disabled people, resulting in a lack of formal qualifications, higher unemployment and social isolation. The rationale for the discussion is also based in the effect of cause and consequence of lack of education among disabled population. Cuong & Mont (2011) notes that in families where a parent is disabled, non-disabled children tend to have lower primary and secondary school participation rates. Part of this is attributed to the fact that in such households, the child's time substitutes for parental time in income generation and household production. It is evident that education is important for disabled people not only for them but also for their next generation, which may be non-disabled.

The outline of the essay is as follows: I will take the problem identified by Case & Taylor (2005), locate the problem within the study of metaphor in linguistics in general and DS in particular, then the measurement of linguistic achievement of children with LD will be reconsidered, taking insights from DS. The acquisition of figurative language in children with LD can be taken as an illustration of the challenges faced by disabled students in normative pedagogy. I will problematise the issue within the discourse of Applied Linguistics and DS paving the way for inclusive education with some suggestions.

Acquisition of Figurative Language in Children with LD: A Case Study

To argue empirically, the process of acquisition of figurative language, especially proverbs in children with LD and the role of cultural experience in cognition will be discussed. Case & Taylor (2005) state that there are more than four million children with LD learn English as a second language (ESL) in the United States. After learning pronunciation and syntactic rules of a language, students with learning disabilities are required to command over the semantics. This leads to the acquisition of proverbs. Research studies have established that understanding of semantic relationships is one of the continuous processes which take years to mature; despite that a student may have a strong control over syntax and pronunciation in ESL (Mercer 1987). However, the acquisition of figurative language in children with LD shows that there is a mismatch between learner's needs and material provided. Case & Taylor argue that such figurative language which involves understanding of semantic relationship demands that students understand language in a variety of communicative functions. Nippold (2000: 24) explains that a proverbs can be used to comment, *Blood is thicker than water*[2]— interpret, *His bark is worse than his bite*— advise, *Don't count your chickens before they are hatched*—or warn, *It is better to be safe than sorry*. Proverbs are one of pragmatic universals of language which are found in across culture. They belong to figurative language, which is rich in semantic relationships, and exist in all languages across the world (ibid), yet mastering their use, as well as the use of metaphors and similes, is particularly difficult for ESL students (Mercer 1987). Proverbs are manifestations of common cultural knowledge realised as collections of short and succinct texts. Their mastery is important for communicative and didactic use of language; however they are condensations of many complex cognitive, linguistic and logico-symbolic operations (Ulatowska et al. 2000). It is also reported that the cultural knowledge contained in proverbs constitutes an essential element of linguistic semantic structure and logical structure of proverbs reveals that there exist definite rules of logical structure of proverbs independent of their semantic meaning (Permyakov 1979; Dundes 1975, cited in Ulatowska et al. 2000).

One of the characteristics of figurative language is metaphors which are a play on linguistic images. They are based on a relationship of similarity between two objects or concepts, that is, based on the same or similar semantic features, which leads to a denotational transfer, e.g., *The clouds are crying* for *It's raining*. A metaphor is also frequently described as a shortened comparison, in which the comparison is nonetheless not explicitly expressed. It may appear in the context of a sentence as nouns, verbs, or adjectives, e.g. *bull's eye* for *point of the target*, *sharp criticism* for *strong criticism*, *to keep one's eyes peeled* for *to watch out for something*. More recent approaches view metaphors

[2] In metaphor scholarship, metaphors are typically represented in all capital letters. However, in Disability Studies, sentences in capital letters are given up in favour of italics to increase accessibility for those who use screen readers, and to reduce the perception of 'yelling.' For this reason, I have not followed the convention of metaphor studies.

not as a purely semantic phenomenon, but rather prefer to view them in connection with their use or establish them at the cognitive, conceptual level. In *Metaphor in Educational Discourse*, Lynne Cameron (2003) explains that Lakoff and Johnson's (1980) cognitive approach to metaphor suggests that 'metaphor is a basic mental operation by which we understand the world through mapping from known domains to unknown domains,' in part because 'some conceptualizations are metaphorically structured in our own minds'.

The role of individual's experience in comprehending a proverb and metaphor has been analysed from a cognitive perspective, which suggests that proverbs function as an automatic pilot of individual thinking. Proverbs place classificatory matrices at our disposal which govern *our experiences* and allow us to form analogies and metaphors (Douglas 1987, cited in Ulatowska et al. 2000, emphasis mine). It is important to note that *our experience* depends on the exposure we have in our environment or surrounding. Ulatowska et al. (2000) again note that 'metaphoricity of proverbs can be perceived intuitively; since proverbs are expressions which inherently contain more information than is possible derivation directly from their structure.' Krikmann (1978) points out that 'these metaphoric meanings of proverbs are canonical and stereotyped, and function to explain what is complex by what is simpler, and what is well-known by what is better known.' It follows, then, that the comprehension of proverbs requires not only the ability to utilise semantic knowledge, but also the ability to manipulate metaphoric analogies which have been transmitted to us by our culture as ready-made interpretative models (Ulatowska et al. 2000).

Research shows that children with LD struggle with the use of figurative language. According to Kuder (2003) students with LD use and understand language with a rigidity that shows up in a number of content areas. In math, for example, if a student with learning disability is asked to make a table using the numbers from a text, he or she may wonder how to make an object with four legs out of numbers. Similarly, for ESL students with LD, the figurative use of language in similes, metaphors, and proverbs also represents a significant challenge. Students with learning disabilities may literally interpret the language, believing that *a bird in the hand is worth two in a bush* is about someone literally holding a bird in his hand (Kuder, cited in Case & Taylor 2005). Case & Taylor conclude the discussion, which explores the overlaps between the characteristics shared by students with learning disabilities and students undergoing the natural process of SLA; calling for more research to be done to unravel the knots surrounding *language difference or disability* (emphasis mine). Taking this concluding remark a step forward, it is required to investigate the phenomenon of *language difference.*

The problem of a normative interpretation of metaphor has been identified by persons with learning disabilities in particular and persons with disabilities in general, which sparked off the debate on language difference vs. disability. The debate can be located in Amy Vidali's (2010), *Seeing What We Know: Disability and Theories of Metaphor.* She quotes Vivian Sobchack (2004) who humorously emphasises that while prosthetic metaphors have become 'a fetishized and "unfleshed-out" catch-word…for a broad and variegated critical discourse on technoculture' (209), such metaphors ignore prosthetic realities. From Sobchack's critique, it can be understood that proverbial and idiomatic construction is an area of concern. These proverbial and idiomatic expressions often contain metaphor which is important, that we often think in metaphoric ways, and that metaphors impact the world, both figuratively and metaphorically. Thus, acquisition of metaphors constitutes the metalinguistic awareness, which any speaker/ learner of a language should be equipped with so the persons with disabilities.

There are proverbs and phrases as well as idioms in languages which are based on ableist experiences and norms. Kumar (2010) analyses a series of dreams on disability in popular dream dictionaries and finds that the interpretations of all these dreams are based on the biased prejudices and stereotypes of disability and questions the 'ableist' interpretations. These biases and prejudices are not just restricted to dreams and their interpretation. Kumar (2011) analyses a set of idiomatic expressions and phrases from Hindi which are formed of '*breaking* of body/ organ/ object' for example, *haath kaTaanaa/ Kaatanaa* (getting hand chopped off/ chopping of hand): to give up or to lose property rights and to snatch another's property respectively, and argued that these proverbs and phrases often carry a negative meaning. Elsewhere I have looked at the 'proverbial wisdom about disabilities' in the proverbs found in Hindustani language (Kumar 2013), for example, *andho me kaana raja* (a one-eyed person is a king among the blind). However, the meaning and the context in which this proverb is said is problematic as it refers to the fact that a semi-literate person would be considered to be a scholar among the illiterate. It is important to note that this proverb carries the prejudice that the 'disabled are inferior' as it equates being blind with being illiterate. It is argued that such proverbial wisdom needs to be critiqued from the disability perspective. I wonder how students, with disabilities in particular and disabled people in general, learn and interpret these linguistic items which are discriminatory and biased in content and form particularly towards them. Disabled students are often taken aback by the use of biased proverbs or idioms in the classroom or elsewhere. In Kumar (2013), I have reported a first person account of a blind research student who faced such awkward moment while participating in the rally. He reacted strongly in one of his mails to a 'basement' reading group SIG-DSU active in Delhi to the use of a slogan, 'We are not blind, VC can't fool us' by fellow protesters. This shows that the use of such biased proverbs either in pedagogy or in daily life is not acceptable to disabled community.

It is a matter of concern that if students with learning disabilities interpret these proverbs literary then there is a great chance of psychological effect on their personalities. Vidali (ibid) reports that disability metaphors can cause such negative consequences even if the person is writing about her/ his own disability, as suggested by G. Thomas Couser (2005) in his critique of Lauren Slater's (2000) *Lying*, which takes epilepsy as a structuring metaphor. He argues that even if Slater has epilepsy, 'her choice of a disability as a metaphor for her experience involves her in a misrepresentation of all those who have that condition' (142), as Slater ultimately equates epilepsy with mental illness and personality disorders (151).

It is really a challenge for learners as well as instructors to interpret the proverbial expressions like, *A blind following a blind*, *There is none so deaf as they that will not hear.* Vidali (2010) presents a disability perspective to explore the ableist nature of metaphor which can be employed to analyse the proverbs as well. She critiques the much celebrated work on metaphor by Lakoff & Johnson (1980) and informs that 'subtle references to able bodies' are found throughout *Metaphors we live by*, including mentions of how 'metaphor pervades our normal conceptual system' (115), the impact on the 'prototypical person' (132), and references to 'natural kinds of experience,' such as 'moving, manipulating objects, eating' (117). It has been argued that such references to 'normal,' 'prototypical,' and 'natural' bodies exclude disabled bodies and experiences. Hence, following Couser (2005), it cannot only be inferred that the proverbial expressions contain biases about disability but also cause some psychological effects.

Vidali's (2010) critique of theories of cognitive metaphor and metaphor acquisition concludes that these theories are *ableist* in assuming that bodies have particular physical/cognitive/sensory experiences and related metaphorical expressions. The possible explanation for the problems that students with LD seem to face in learning this aspect of language could be that since students with LD do not match the experience expressed in metaphorical language, they are unable to comprehend the task. However, even other disabled people, such as the visually impaired and hearing impaired may be able to only conceptually comprehened such concepts because it is difficult for them to view the world from others (ableist) perspectives because they may experience the world in different and innovative ways. It is possible that the children with learning disabilities in particular, and disabled people in general, have their roots in cultures that are markedly different from normative culture. They may have their own unique experiences of spatiality, moral values, social ethos, or the network human relationships. Language educators need to appreciate this difference in experience and design the pedagogy in such a holistic way that include some contents from disability studies as well.

Interrogating the Measurement of Linguistic Achievement

To validate the proposal outlined above, it is required to interrogate the measurement of linguistic achievement. This provides another reason for necessary change in language pedagogy of inclusive education. It has been a common practice across the disciplines to measure the achievement of learners against some standard. However, the *standard* has always been that of the majority view of society. Simi Linton (2010), a disabled women advocate and one of the pioneers of DS, in her essay *Disability Studies/ Not Disability Studies*, has raised the case that disabled people's achievement, whether linguistic or otherwise, is measured on the scales of normal people and on account of their below par achievement, they are viewed as a problem. She elaborates this in terms of the prevalence of biological determinism, 'Education, clinical psychology and other social sciences have been particularly influential in reinforcing these deterministic views. These fields conceptualize disability as deviance from the norm, as pathological condition and as deficit, and concentrate their efforts on the evaluation of these individual characteristics' (ibid).

Ulatowska et al. (2000) states that in general, metaphoric expressions have been used to study cognitive function (Buehler 1907; Piaget 1923; Benjamin 1944), thought processes (Goldstein & Scheerer 1941, 1973; Wechsler 1955 cited in Ulatowska et al. 2000) and also assessment of intellectual development in children (Piaget 1923, 1969) in Psychology. It is clear from the goal of these studies that as Ulatowska et al. observe, 'In psychiatric, neurological, and psychological diagnosis, proverbs are believed to assess the mental status of patients and their ability to think abstractly and to describe and categorize impairments in those areas.' In the tradition of the neurologist Goldstein, the ability to grasp abstraction was considered to be a sign of normalcy, while concretism of interpretation was considered a sign of pathology or ageing (Goldstein & Scheerer 1941). However, the aim of this approach facilitates the general principles of the subject in relation to specific tasks of intervention and material production (Crystal 1984). Though, these models work on the underlying principle of intervention and individualise disability, Shakespeare (2007) finds that, 'Despite the deficiencies of medical sociology and medical ethics, it would be foolish to ignore the many valuable contributions to understanding disability made from these perspectives.' The findings obtained from these researches have contributed to the field of special education. However, it is important to note that none of these measurement tools accord equality to both the abled and disabled.

Disability, Disability Studies and Its Insights and Applied Linguistics

There is a growing interest in and increased visibility of the field of DS both in and out of the disability community. Linton (2010) provides a coherent rationale for marking a border that sets off Disability Studies as a socio-political-cultural examination of disability, which is different from the traditional study of disability based on interventionist approaches. She also cites one of the major problems in the current presentation of disability, predominantly in rehabilitation and in special education, is individualising disability—the curriculum fosters the idea that disability is an individual's or at most a family's problem.' The absence of disability discourse has been deeply regretted in multicultural curricula. As Linton (2010) regrets, throughout the curriculum there is insufficient attention to disabled people as a minority group, and the cultural, political, and intellectual meanings of that status. Furthermore, diversity initiatives and multicultural curriculum endeavours have, for the most part, ignored disability as a category of analysis. Though, there have been a number of studies on language and education, there is little available work which considers 'disability' as a variable, a factor or as a category of analysis throughout the literature, except the works in psycholinguistics and neurolinguistics that are again problematic from the perspective of Disability Studies as they fall in the traditional canon of medicalisation of disability. Linton notes that this results into a pathologising of difference, the individualisation of disability, a loss of self-definition and self-determination, a forced assignment of the role of patient, client and consumer.

Disability movements in India have enjoyed some significant springs, they have largely been rights-based. Nilika Mehrotra (2011) sets to map out the 'chequered history of the disability rights movements in India by referring to the social and political contexts, within which they emerged, the ideological influences, structures, issues, possibilities and challenges.' She reports that critics of disability movements maintain that efforts are being directed towards development of infrastructure and not towards conducive interpretation of disability in the Indian context (Mehrotra 2006, 2008; Miles 2002; Staples 2007). Nikhil Jain (2011) presents a commentary on the state of affairs regarding accessibility in the campuses of universities in Delhi. He regrets that 'University campuses in Delhi continue to be ill-equipped physically and academically to deal with issues related to the disabled.' He notes that, '[t]here are other social and pedagogically related barriers. The paucity of reading material in accessible form for the visually impaired in DU.' Mehrotra (ibid) summarises, 'In India, the provision of accessible environment, disability support services, job reservation and rights issues have to be contextualised within the larger picture of deprivation and marginalisation.'

However, it is Tanmoy Bhattacharya (2010) who raises the issues of inclusion in his analytical essay, 'Re-examining issue of inclusion in education in real sense'. He highlights that the condition for inclusion to work is 'curriculum content, rather than merely curriculum delivery, must change where the child's right to belong to a mainstream school does not remain a matter of legal right but becomes their moral and political right.' His emphasis on 'curriculum content' should be noted down in earnest. Though he talks about the curriculum of education in general, it can easily refer to language pedagogy. It is worth noting that while disability rights movements articulate the demand for disability-friendly pedagogy in *form* in terms of accessibility, they are often unable to understand the need for disability-friendly pedagogy in *content*. It is therefore proposed that there should be a structural change in pedagogy in terms of both form and content.

Though, the research in Second Language Acquisition and its recognition of the needs of marginalised learners is path-breaking, yet the absence of disabled people as a political category shows the invisibility of disabled people from the imagination of masses as well as classes. Except for persons with learning disabilities, such as Autistic and hearing/ speech impairment, other disabled people such as visually-challenged and physically challenged are *adjusted* to the mainstream schools rather than *adjusting* the schools to the needs of the former till recent times. Agnihotri, Khanna, & Sachdev (1998: 24) conclude with the hope that 'future research, employing novel methodologies, may be able to capture a more holistic approach to second language learning than has been the case so far.' Taking this as a point of departure, I propose that second language learning in particular and education in general should be based on a holistic approach which should include the communicative needs of disabled learners.

Language teaching, which has been a central theme of Applied Linguistics, can address the urgency of inclusion of disabled students in mainstream school. Language plays an important role not only in language as subject but also as a medium of expression. Agnihotri & Khanna (1994: 9) have this to say about the autonomous status of Applied Linguistics, 'It applies insights not only from the theories of general linguistics but also from the (sic) several other disciplines to practical problems connected with language.' Taking cues from the above, it is proposed that Applied Linguistics must accept the challenge and insights of DS. It will serve two purposes: first, Applied Linguistics can process information on and about 'disability' from the perspective of Disability Studies to develop its own theoretical models of language pedagogy in inclusive education. Second, it may also help us to clear the confusion about the nature of language and principles of language learning resulting from mere speculation of the medical model adopted in Psycholinguistics and Neurolinguistics.

Inclusive Education

This discussion aims to contribute to inclusive education. The talk over inclusive education stepped up with the enactment of the Right of Children to Free and Compulsory Education Act, 2009. In this context, the right to education of children with disabilities has raised questions which needs to be assessed. Bhattacharya (2010) observes that the philosophy behind inclusive schools is that all children have the right to be educated with their peers in regular classrooms in neighbourhood schools. Moreover, the concept of

'Inclusive education' advocates an intrinsic respect for difference, thereby celebrating diversity rather than creating labels that delimit human potential. Inclusion is considered to be a dynamic process that implies changes in school ethos to create a community that accepts and values difference (Oliver 1996).

Agnihotri & Khanna (1995), while setting the tone of ELT in the Indian context, forward a rich argument in favour of the multilingual experiences of Indian society; the same argument can be solicited in favour of the experiences of disabled community. 'If we want Indian students to learn English to acquire the ability to negotiate day-to-day social encounters demanding the use of English and the ability to read texts critically in a socio-historical context' then I add to this, it would be unfair to expect children with disabilities to do the 'same' according to ableist norms of the society. Again, Bhattacharya (2010) notes the confusion over the two semantically proximate terms—inclusion and integration—needs to be resolved because it aggravates with other variants of integration (geographical, social, and functional); though all forms of integration are a matter of location, they all also have the common assumption of assimilation (of the child with disability into the mainstream school). He further notes that the result of this is the emergence of the philosophy of integration, that is, of the child fitting in, whereas the school remain largely unchanged. Taking this analysis as an analogy for language education of children with disabilities, I would like say that the philosophy of integration seems to be overshadowing the different innovative teaching methodologies which have been devised to 'fit' the child in, whereas the contents of the pedagogy remain unchanged. Thus, the philosophy of inclusion needs to be focused on content as well as in language pedagogy.

Language Teaching in Inclusive Education

Agnihotri & Khanna (1995: 12) outline the goal of language education as follows: 'A critical awareness about language structure, its role in society and the development of critical faculties of the learner should constitute the goals of language teaching.'

This is followed by a suggestion for this reconceptualisation of language proficiency in multilingual situations which involve a reallocation of our educational resources. This can be applicable in inclusive education as well if we replace the term 'multilingual' with 'multicultural', since disabled students constitute a culture of difference which needs to be celebrated. Agnihotri & Khanna (1995: 13) argue strongly to maximise gains on the richness of experiences of multilingual societies: 'It should be possible to cultivate metalinguistic awareness among children through a comparative and cognitively challenging study of languages in *their* repertoire.' It is, thus, argued that gains should be capitalised on the richness of experiences of multiculturalism in the class.

Simi Linton (2010) calls for a revamping of the approaches to disability from applied fields and urges us to 'develop more valid and useful approaches to the presence of impairment in the population and disability in society, and respond to disabled people in a less deterministic and in a more integrated way than the applied fields ever have. Although the focus of the applied fields is on individual interventions, research and curricula should carefully examine the contextual variables that shape experience.' She also suggests that the voice of disabled people will help to remove the absence of subjectivity in scholarship. This can be done by adopting writings of disabled people into curricula. Lessons can be learnt from Women's Studies which have changed the academic curriculum to reveal the epistemological consequences of androcentric biases in the knowledge base (Linton 2010). Bhattacharya (2010) suggests from (Rieser 2006) curriculum restructuring must be done to include disability issues and positive portrayal of people with disability in a non-patronising manner and in non-stereotyped activities and roles. This will have a double benefit, first, it will make curricula contextually and culturally sensitive for disabled learners, and second, it will help to create awareness among mainstream learners. It is also to be noted that suggestion to prepare pedagogies based on the experience of disability will help to create awareness among abled-bodied persons from the beginning. It should be remembered that 'effective pedagogy for students with disability is effective pedagogy for all students' (Adams and Brown 2006).

Recommendations

It becomes clear from the above discussion that education in general, and language teaching in particular, for persons with disabilities needs to be appropriated to the experiences of disabled community. It should be seen as an integral part of the curriculum and participate in the processes of social change. I believe that the teacher or instructor plays an important role in interpreting the proverbs in question. It is the teacher who serves as a 'vicarious consciousness' (Bruner 1985), sharing the burden of learning with the student and reducing the complexity of the task to be mastered in order to allow the learner to concentrate on the critical features. However, there may be some logical constraints as the demographical distribution of disabled people in a geographically vast country like India. The paucity of audio-visual aids, shortage of trained human resource, the attitudinal barriers of normal people etc., may be overcome if policies and pedagogies are implemented with an earnest effort. The following recommendations can be considered while preparing language pedagogy for inclusive education.

1. A lesson can be learnt from the contextualisation of Second Language Acquisition in India and Special Education. I suggest that the existing teaching material should be modified in consonance with the needs of children with disabilities. The communicative needs of learners, alternative curriculum and syllabus design, material selection and the role of various social and psychological variables should be borne in mind while thinking about education for disabled people in general. As A. S. Gupta (1995) suggests, the content of the selected texts should be closely related to the child's socio-cultural experience. It is important to note that the socio-cultural experience of the disabled learner ought to be different, as they perceive and experience the world differently. A lesson from special education suggests the same, as Victoria Risko (1981) reported long back with reference to language acquisition in children with LD in special education. She points out, 'Language learning occurs in social systems, with students' experiences providing a basis for understanding.' The

nature and quality of children's early linguistic environment is probably the external factor that affects the rate of language development (McCarthy 1954; Schiefelbusch 1967, cited in Risko 1981). Smith (1975) also reports that students' cognitive structures organise and summarise experiences and knowledge. Risko (1981: 180) observes on above finding that, it is important to present information in a form consistent with the knowledge and experiential level of students.

2. Pedagogy for figurative language for the metalinguistic achievement of disabled students should be prepared using the disability approach and reinterpreted in a creative and historical way. As Vidali (2010) proposes, a disability approach to metaphor that engages the diversity of disability; refrains from policing metaphor; encourages transgression from the disability community; and invites creative and historical reinterpretations of metaphor. Patrick, J. Devlieger (1999) presents a set of proverbs as texts that can be deciphered for larger frames of reference of personhood and cosmogony. He stresses that culturally-sensitive education of persons with disabilities may include an analysis of the images and discourses developed in a culture, including an analysis of disability as metaphor. It is argued that disabled persons who master such knowledge may be in a position to more clearly understand what cultural material has been developed about them and may build up the skills to work with this material in their daily lives and, if necessary, build a resistance against such material (Devlieger ibid). It is important to talk about those biased forms of language as Bhattacharya (2010) cautions against the 'blackening out' by non-inclusion of disability issues and disabled people, which is a more dangerous form of denial of rightful location in culture. Much of popular media and literature is equally guilty of this denial.
3. It will be a challenge for instructors as they have to take a neutral stance while explaining these metaphorically loaded proverbs and idioms in terms of recent development in disability studies.

4. A word of caution can avoid a crisis. Kauffman et al. (2004) show concerns over shifting towards full inclusion and accommodation. As the authors express, 'The emphasis in special education has shifted away from a normalization, independence, and competence. The result has been student's dependence on whatever special programs, modifications and accommodations are possible, particularly in general education settings. The goal seems to have become the *appearance* of normalisation without the *expectation* of competence (2004, emphasis is original). I think this is a genuine concern raised by the authors which deserves due attention while preparing pedagogical material.
5. The presence of a sign language interpreter and material in Braille should be provided in classes of inclusive education because of the phonocentric and visual mode of language in the case of deaf and visually impaired learners respectively. The presence of a sign language interpreter in the inclusive classroom is necessary. Researches show that mother tongue instruction can enhance the rate of learning. For example, Nadkarni (1994) reports that 'the mother tongue enthusiasts who have dealt exclusively on the psychological, emotional and cultural benefit of mother tongue medium schools have strengthened the view that English can be learnt adequately only if it is the medium of instruction' (as summarised in Agnihotri & Khanna 1994: 6).

Conclusion

The essay concludes with the suggestion that these metaphoric and proverbial expressions should be taught with utmost sensitivity to students with learning disabilities so they can be good at language use in different contexts. In the process, this essay explores a way of language teaching in inclusive education. The discussion arose from the debate on language difference vs. disability. Gaining insights from disability studies, which suggest that disabled people constitutes a culture of difference, and the role of socio-culture perspective in language teaching, it is suggested that language teaching not only provide accessible *form* of material in the physical sense but also in *content*, according to cultural and cognitive sense in inclusive education. If we give weight to the cognitive abilities of children with normal abilities in learning grammar (Raina & Agnihotri 1995), then, I add, we should be more considerate with regards to the children with learning disabilities in particular and disabled children in general. It is accepted that more research needs to be done to unravel the intricacies surrounding language difference or disability but for that inclusive education and pedagogy are required to validate this point.

References

Agnihotri, R. K. & A. L Khanna, (eds), (1994). *Second Language Acquisition: Socio-cultural and Linguistic Aspect of English in India*. New Delhi, Thousand Oaks, London: Sage Publications.

——— (1995). *English Language Teaching in India: Issues and Innovations*. New Delhi, Thousand Oaks, London: Sage Publications.

Agnihotri, R. K., A. L. Khanna, & I. Sachdev (eds), (1998). *Social Psychological Perspectives on Second Language Learning*. New Delhi, Thousand Oaks, London: Sage Publications.

Adams, Mike & Sally Brown (eds), (2006). *Towards Inclusive Learning in Higher Education: Developing Curricula for Disabled Students*. Oxford: Routledge.

Bhattacharya, Tanmoy, (2010). 'Re-examining issue of inclusion in education'. *Economic & Political Weekly*, XLV/ 16, 18–25.

Barnes, Colin, (1991). *Disabled People in Britain and Discrimination*. London: Hurst.

——— (1993). 'Political correctness, language and rights'. *Rights Not Charity*, 1, 8.

Bruner, J. S., (1985). 'Vygotsky: A historical and conceptual perspective'. In J.V. Wertsch (ed.), *Culture, Communication & Cognition: Vygotskian Perspectives.* Cambridge: Cambridge University Press.

Cameron, Lynne, (2003). *Metaphor in Educational Discourse.* London: Continuum.

Case, Rod E. & Shanon, S. Taylor, (2005). 'Language difference or learning disability? Answers from a linguistic perspective'. *The Clearing House*, 78/ 3, 127–30.

Conrad, R., (1979). *The Deaf School Child*. London: Harper & Row.

Corker, Mairian, (2010). 'Disability politics, language planning and inclusive social policy'. *Disability & Society*, 15/ 3, 445–62.

Cuong, Nguyen Viet, & Daniel Mont, (2011). 'Does parental disability matter to child education?' World Bank Policy Research Working Paper, No. 5743.

Couser, G. Thomas, (2005). 'Disability as metaphor: What's wrong with lying.' *Prose Studies*, 27/ 1–2, 141–54.

Crystal, David, (1984). *Linguistic Encounters with Language Handicap*. Basil Blackwell: Oxford.

Devlieger, Patrick J., (1999). 'Frames of reference in African proverbs on disability'. *International Journal of Disability, Development and Education*, 46/ 4, 439–51.

Douglas, M., (1987). *Ainsi Pensent les Institutions* (*Thus Think Institutions*). Paris: Usher.

Dundes, A., (1975). 'On the structure of the proverb'. *Proverbium: Yearbook of International Proverb Scholarship*, 25, 961–73.

Gibbs, R. W., (1994). *The Poetics of Mind: Figurative Thought, Language, and Understanding.* New York: Cambridge University Press.

Goldstein, K. & M. Scheerer, (1941). 'Abstract and concrete behavior: An experimental study with special tests'. *Psychological Monographs*, 53/ 2, no. 239.

Gupta, Anju. S., (1995). 'Medium of instruction in a multilingual context.' In R. K. Agnihotri & A. L. Khanna (eds), *English Language Teaching in India: Issues and Innovations*. New Delhi, Thousand Oaks, London: Sage Publications, 201–11.

Honeck, R. P. & J. G. Temple, (1994). 'Proverbs: The extended conceptual base and great chain metaphor theories'. *Metaphor and Symbolic Activity*, 9, 85–112.

Honeck, R. P., K. Voegtle, M. A. Dorfmueller, & R. R. Hoffman, (1980). 'Proverbs, meaning and group structure'. In R. P. Honeck & R. R. Hoffman (eds), *Cognition and Figurative Language*. Hillsdale, New York: Lawrence Erlbaum Associates, 127–61.

Jain, Nikhil, (2011). 'Addressing concerns of the disabled in Delhi campuses'. *Economic & Political Weekly*, XLVI/50, 19–20.

Kalyanpur, Maya, (2008). 'The paradox of majority underrepresentation in special education in India'. *The Journal of Special Education*, 42/1, 55–64.

Kauffman, James M., Kathleen McGee & Michele Brigham, (2004). 'Enabling or disabling? Observations on changes in special education'. *The Phi Delta Kappan*, 85/8, 613–20.

Krikmann, A. A., (1978). 'Nekotorye aspekty semanticheskoi neopredelennosti poslovitsy' (Some aspects of semantic undefiniteness of proverb). In G. L. Permyakov (ed.) *Paremiologichesky Sbornik. Poslovitsa, Zagadka (Struktura, Smysl, Tekst) [Paremiological Anthology. Proverb, Riddle (Structure, Meaning, Text)]*. Moscow: Nauka Publishing House, 82–104.

Kuder, S. J., (2003). *Teaching Students with Language and Communication Disabilities*, 2nd Edn. Boston: Pearson Education.

Kumar, Santosh, (2013). 'Proverbial wisdom about persons with disabilities'. J. Rui, Outi and Lauhakangas (eds), 6th Interdisciplinary Colloquium on Proverbs/IPC12 Proceedings. Tavira, Patugal, 260–72.

——— (2012). 'Tabooed cups and chipped phrases: An enquiry into the negative interpretation of disability'. Paper at Three-day Conference on Interrogating Disability: Theory and Practice, Institute of Development Studies, Kolkata, 27–29 September.

——— (2011). '(Linguistic) Disablism in the psychological dreams interpretations'. Paper at Exploring Disability Experience in Social Science Research, Centre for the Study of Social Systems, School of Social Sciences, JNU, New Delhi, 25–26 March.

Lakoff, George & Mark Johnson, (1980). *Metaphors We Live By*. Chicago, IL, London: University of Chicago.

Levine, E. S., (1981). *The Ecology of Early Deafness: Guides to Fashioning Environments and Psychological Assessments*. New York: Columbia University Press.

Linton, Simi, (2010). 'Disability studies/Not disability studies'. *Disability and Society*, 13/4, 535–39.

McCarthy, D., (1954). 'Language disorders and parent-child relationships'. *Journal of Speech and Hearing Disorder*, 19, 514–23.

Mehrotra, Nilika, (2011). 'Disability rights movements in India: Politics and practice'. *Economic & Political Weekly*, XLVI/ 6, 65–72.

——— (2006). 'Negotiating gender and disability in rural Haryana'. *Sociological Bulletin*, 55/3, 406–26.

Mehrotra, Raja Ram, (1995). 'Literary bias in teaching of English as a second language'. In R. K. Agnihotri & A. L. Khanna (eds), *English Language Teaching in India: Issues and Innovations*. New Delhi, Thousand Oaks, London: Sage Publications, 105–15.

Menon, Nidhiya, Susan Parish & Roderick Rose, (2012). 'The "state" of persons with disabilities in India'. A working paper.

Mieder, W., (1993). 'Proverbs are never out of season: Popular wisdom in the modern age'. New York: Oxford University Press.

Miles, M., (2002). 'Community and individual responses to disablement in South Asian histories: Old traditions, new myths?' http://www.independentsliving.org/doc3nites2002a.html. Last accessed 4 October 2016.

Mercer, C. D., (1987). *Students with Learning Disabilities*, 3rd Edn. Columbus, OH: Merrill.

Nadkarni, M. V., (1994). 'English in mother tongue medium education'. In R. K. Agnihotri & R. L Khanna (eds), *Second Language Acquisition: Socio Cultural and Linguistic Aspect of English in India*. New Delhi, Thousand Oaks, London: Sage Publications, 130–42.

Narula, S. C., (1995). 'Use of Indian culture and myth in ELT'. In R. K. Agnihotri & A. L. Khanna (eds), *English Language Teaching in India: Issues and Innovations*. New Delhi/ Thousand Oaks/ London: Sage Publications, 116–27.

National Sample Survey Organisation, (2002). Data on the literary rate among disabled people.

Nippold, M. A., (2000). 'Language development during the adolescent years: Aspects of pragmatics, syntax and semantics'. *Topics in Language Disorders*, 20/2, 15–28 February.

Oliver, Mike, (1996). *Understanding Disability*. Basingstoke: Macmillan.

Piaget, J., (1923). 'La pense!e symbolique et la pense!e de l'enfant' (Symbolic thought and thought of the child). *Archives Psychology*, 18, 273–304.

——— (1969). *Language and Thought in the Child*. New York: Basic Books.

Permyakov, G. L. (1979). *From Proverb to Folk-tale: Notes on the General Theory of Cliché*. Moscow: Nauka Publishing House.

Raina, A. S. & R. K. Agnihotri, (1995). 'Grammar, cognitive abilities and second language learning'. In R. K. Agnihotri & A. L. Khanna (eds), *English Language Teaching in India: Issues and Innovations*. New Delhi/ Thousand Oaks/ London: Sage Publications, 242–58.

Rieser, Richard, (2006). 'Inclusive education or special educational needs'. In Mike Cole (ed.), *Education, Equality, and Human Rights: Issues of Gender, 'Race', Sexuality, Disability and Social Class*. Oxford: Routledge, 157–79.

Risko, Victoria, (1981). 'Oral language'. In Deborah Deutsch Smith (ed.), *Teaching the Learning Disabled*, NJ: Prentice-Hall, Inc.

Schiefelbusch, R. L., (1967). 'The development of communication skills'. In R. L. Schiefelbusch, R. H. Copeland, & J. O. Smith (eds), *Language and Mental Retardation: Emperical and Conceptual Considerations*. New York: Holt, Rinehart & Winston.

Slater, Lauren., (2000). *Lying*. New York: Random House.

Smith, F., (1975). *Comprehension and Learning: A Conceptual Framework for Teachers*. New York: Hort, Rinehart & Winston.

Sobchack, Vivian, (2004). *Carnal Thoughts: Embodiment and Moving in Image Culture*. Berkeley: University of California Press.

Staples, James, (2007). *Peculiar People, Amazing Lives: Leprosy, Social Exclusion and Community Making in South India*. Delhi: Orient Longman.

'The right of children to free and compulsory education act, 2009'. (2009). In, the *Extraordinary Gazette of India*. New Delhi: Ministry of Law and Justice, Government of India.

The 15th Census of India 2011. (2011). Government of India. India.

The United Nations Convention on the Rights of Persons with Disabilities, (2006).

Thomas, Phillipa. (2005). 'Mainstreaming disability in development: India country Report'. Disability Knowledge and Research Report. http://worldbank.org/INSTSARREGTOPLASSOCPRO/.../IndiaReportPHD.pdf. Last accessed on 3.10.2016.

Touraine, Allen, (2009). *Thinking Differently* (trans. David Macey), Cambridge, UK: Polity Press.

Ulatowska, H. K. M., Sadowska, D. Kadzielawa, J. Kordy, & K. Rymarczyk, (2000). 'Linguistic and cognitive aspects of proverb processing in aphasia'. *Aphasiology*, 14/3, 227–50.

Vanikar, Ranu V. & Katayun K. Palia, (1995). 'The tailor's dummy: The influence of cultural content of ESL Materials on learner output'. In R. K. Agnihotri and A. L. Khanna (eds), *English Language Teaching in India: Issues and Innovations*. New Delhi, Thousand Oaks, London: Sage Publications, 128–38.

Vidali, Amy, (2010). 'Seeing what we know: disability and theories of metaphor'. *Journal of Literary & Cultural Disability Studies*, 4/1, 33–54.

Wechsler, D., (1955). *Wechsler Adult Intelligence Scale*. New York: Psychological Corporation.

Disability in India—A statistical profile, March 2011, Central Statistics office, Ministry of Statistics & Program Implementation, Government of India, cited in Shenoy, Meera (2011) 'Persons with disability & the india labour market: challenges and opportunities'. December 2011, http: //www.ilo.org/wcmsp5/groups/public/---asia/---ro-bangkok/---sro-new_delhi/documents/publication/wcms_229259.pdf. Last accessed on 18 March 2016.

CHAPTER 14

Language Teaching and Learning for Children with Autism Spectrum Disorder

SHUBHANGI VAIDYA AND MERRY BARUA

Abstract

Autism Spectrum Disorder (ASD) is a lifelong developmental disorder characterised by impairments in the areas of language, social behaviour and imagination, and is the consequence of atypical brain development. Its early signs and symptoms are noticed around the second year of a child's life, which in the case of typically developing children is a period of immense growth and development in language, communication and learning of social skills. As ASD is a spectrum disorder with varying degrees of severity and differences in manifestation or presentation, children with mild to moderate impairments frequently find themselves in 'regular' classrooms where they are expected to learn and perform like their typically developing peers. When they are unable to cope, their difficulties are frequently dismissed as 'bad behaviour' or they are termed as 'spoilt brats'. This paper attempts to outline the 'red flags' or symptoms that indicate the presence of Autism and help teachers to devise ways and means of helping these children to integrate in the classroom setting. It specifically focuses on strategies of language teaching and learning which lie at the core of ASD. These strategies will not only benefit children with disability but will also foster good teaching learning practices in 'mainstream' settings.

INTRODUCTION

Autism Spectrum Conditions, more commonly referred to as Autism Spectrum Disorders, is a complex neuro-developmental condition which has emerged as a major public health challenge across the world. First described as a distinct syndrome by the Austrian psychiatrist Leo Kanner in 1943, it has captured the imagination of neuro-scientists, psychiatrists, social scientists and educationists alike. With the advances in scientific knowledge about the condition, diagnosis and assessment has also become more nuanced and sophisticated, with the result that the number of persons diagnosed has increased exponentially. The latest figures from the Centres of Disease Control in the USA suggest that 1 out of every 50 school-going children in the USA is likely to be on the 'autism spectrum'. Even though we have no definite statistics for India, going by the prevalence rate worldwide, it is estimated that ten million individuals are likely to have autism. This chapter aims to familiarise teachers with the characteristics associated with Autism Spectrum Conditions in order to enable them to understand in a better way the difficulties in learning experienced by such children who may be in their classrooms. It is expected that this will help teachers devise and implement classroom strategies that will facilitate teaching and learning. Along with social understanding, the areas of language and communication present special difficulties to students with autism. In this chapter we shall concentrate specifically on the latter.

Children with autism often have a different way of learning. However, they all have the ability to learn and benefit from learning in a regular classroom when the environment is accommodating and non-judgmental. While individuals with some disabilities require physical prostheses, for individuals with autism the main prostheses are attitude and understanding.

We will begin by examining Autism Spectrum Conditions and focus upon the core differences in development in language and communication that characterise the condition. We will then attempt to understand how these differences can be accommodated within the classroom setting and how appropriate strategies and supports can facilitate a more wholesome and rewarding teaching-learning experience.

Understanding Autism

Autism is a life-long neuro-developmental condition that affects areas of social interaction, language and social communication, and flexibility of thought and imagination. In addition, persons with autism often face challenges in processing sensory input leading to hypersensitivity or hyposensitivity to stimuli such as light, sound, vision, hearing or touch, and dealing with proprioceptive and vestibular input. This can affect the way they respond to the environment resulting sometimes in rocking, flapping of hands, finger flicking, looking through the sides of their eyes, or sniffing objects. While such behaviours often seem odd, they are a reflection of a physical need within the person and enable them to process the world better.

Persons with autism are believed to have difficulties in 'theory of mind' functions, i.e., the ability to comprehend the mental states of others and orient behaviour accordingly (Frith 1989 cited in Jordan 1997). We make predictions about the behaviour of other people based upon our understandings of their thoughts, feelings and intentions. An inability to figure out these mental states will lead to difficulty in predicting behaviour, and this in turn will mean that people may appear unpredictable or even frightening.

Even when they understand that others are talking about them in 'not-nice' ways, they do not understand the reasons, or what they can do about it. Similarly, when they talk only about things of their interests, they are unable to 'guess' that other people might be getting bored. A typically developing child will tease another child only when the teacher is not looking. This is because they 'know' that if the teacher sees them, the child will be punished. Persons with autism do not have this understanding. Therefore, when some other child teases them, they retaliate in public, without trying to hide, and get into trouble. Most do not know how to lie.

Persons with autism have difficulties with executive functioning such as planning, monitoring and directing activities, reflecting on one's mental states and using flexible means to achieve goals, and using past and present experience to solve problems. This is the reason why many children do not understand and learn when punished or when people say 'no'. As a result, when reprimanded they do not know what they are expected to do in place of what they were already doing. Instead they end up indulging in rituals, repetitive actions or activities that generate predictability; and are often labelled stubborn, disobedient, inattentive and rude.

While in coming years a wider spectrum of children will seek admission in regular classrooms, currently the children who are likely to find themselves in your classroom will in all probability be those with either high-functioning autism (HFA) or Asperger's Syndrome (AS). Persons with AS are often highly verbal yet socially naïve individuals who share the same core difficulties in social understanding as other persons on the spectrum. Many go undiagnosed as they seem so 'normal'; paradoxically, this often leads to merciless teasing, bullying and a resultant lack of self-esteem, as the biological condition underlying their behaviour is neither acknowledged or understood. If you look back at your own experiences as teachers, many of you are bound to recall the odd, withdrawn, aloof child who simply did not 'fit in' with the lively environment of the classroom, or the awkward 'little professor' who was a walking encyclopaedia but did not know how to make friends and was often considered 'rude' and 'snooty'. It is quite likely that some of these children may have met the diagnostic criteria for autism or Asperger's Syndrome.

Language and Communication Difficulties in Autism

Autism is a 'spectrum disorder' ranging from individuals who may pass as merely odd or eccentric to those with severe difficulties in daily functioning who may need life-long care; and from those who do not speak to those who display complex, grammatically correct speech. Some individuals may show only slight delays in language and greater difficulties in making friends. Some may have no sensory difficulties while for others every day has too much sensory information. However, each person has his or her own strengths, and challenges and like all individuals, each person with autism has a unique personality and combination of characteristics.

The following explain some of the common challenges faced.

- Understanding non-verbal communication. For instance, deriving meaning from a teacher's sudden silence accompanied by a steady gaze in the student's direction (and therefore quickly returning to one's seat/ sitting down/ stopping chatter with one's neighbour etc.); the child may not understand that the teacher is angry.
- Spontaneously using non-speech communication such as looking into the teacher's eyes when speaking to him/ her, exhibiting an expression of regret when being reprimanded (whether experiencing a feeling of regret or not!), conveying pleasure, gratitude, anxiety etc. through facial expressions, and generally using face and body to communicate, raising hands to give an answer in class, looking towards the teacher to draw attention to self in order to speak.
- A vocabulary which may be restricted to nouns, limited in social functions and confined to requests to regulate the physical environment.
- Sharing and recounting experiences, achievements, emotions.
- Understanding that a narration must provide context for those who do not know the background.
- Understanding that communication has to be interpreted in context and has a meaning beyond the literal. For example when told to 'Take a seat', one has to sit and not pick up a chair. Or calling someone 'crazy' with an accompanying smile means something different from when it is said without a smile; that the accompanying tone of voice and the facial expression tells us the speaker's intent.
- Deriving meaning from prosody. For instance understanding from her/ his tonal inflection whether the teacher's 'Do you want to finish your work' was a command, a rebuke or a question.

- Understanding and detecting the presence of sarcasm in the speaker's words and tone.
- Speaking in a flat tone, or with a singsong delivery, too loud or too soft.
- Establishing a mutual or shared focus of attention.
- Repetitive or idiosyncratic speech patterns.
- Echoing a question as a response, for example, answering 'Have you completed your homework?' with 'Completed your homework'.
- Recalling long verbal instructions.
- Perseverating on a topic, i.e. continually discussing a particular topic and having difficulty in moving to the next one.
- Difficulty with pragmatics of communication (initiating and maintaining a conversation, inappropriate interrupting, stereotypic or inflexible style of speaking). (Adapted from *Teaching Students with Autism: A Resource Guide for Schools*, Ministry of Education, Special Programs Branch, British Columbia: 2000)

It will be apparent to you that the autistic mind processes information differently. Some of the challenges of language-based learning arise out of their difficulties in using theory of mind. As teachers, it is important to note that most students with autism will have difficulties in comprehending verbal information, long strings of verbal instructions as well as complex sequences of instruction. They may find it difficult to hold on to information received aurally. Persons with autism tend to be 'visual learners' who learn better when instructions are presented visually: as written words, or through graphics. Visual information is enduring and more concrete, unlike speech which is ephemeral. Moreover, using visual instructions and cues in the classroom benefits not just the child with autism but also ALL learners.

There are a few basic rules in communicating with persons with autism that can prove equally effective with other students in your classroom.

1. The word 'Don't!' is used more frequently than we realise. Yet, it really does not clarify what we want our learner to do! Wherever possible, tell the learner what she is supposed

to do, rather than what she is not supposed to. For instance, saying 'Don't throw the paper on the floor!' only tells the child what she just did. Telling her to pick it up and throw it in the waste paper basket indicates what behaviour is expected of her. 'I want you to behave yourself,' does not tell the child what is expected of him; 'Sit on your chair. (pause) Fold your arms,' does. In the same vein, reprimands and threats do not guide the child towards desired behaviours and instead give importance to undesired behaviours.

2. Secure the child's attention prior to communicating by calling his name, or by physically prompting (e.g. touching his shoulder). 'Somi! Pick up that paper and throw it in the waste basket.'
3. Use language that is clear, precise and simple.
4. Reduce the amount of auditory information given. Use simple short sentences. Break a long instruction into short instructions. If you want the child to 'take his bag and go for music', say, 'Put your books in. Stand. Take your bag. Go to the music room.' Saying, 'Finish the Q and A. Take out the Grammar workbook. Open to page 45. Complete exercises 1 to 5,' with brief pauses will be far more effective than 'Finish the Q and A, go to page 45 in the grammar workbook and do exercises A and B.' Another way would be to write the instructions on the board: 'Grammar Workbook, Page 45, Ex 1–5'.
5. Teach the child to listen. By following through an instruction with actions that will ensure compliance, the meaningfulness of language is established. Say, 'Ronit, take out your math exercise book'. Wait a moment and give time for processing the instruction. If need be, repeat the instruction one more time and simultaneously physically guide the child into taking out the book. This ensures that the child learns to listen and follow directions instead of failing constantly in compliance. Consistency on the part of the adult is the key to helping the child learn to listen and comply.
6. Be very clear about what you want the learner to do and why. Use specific instructions rather than the abstract. Say

'Keep it on the table,' rather than 'Keep it there'; or 'Finish your written work. Then we will have a break' is much more specific and has clear-cut expectations rather than 'We will have a break when you are ready'.

7. Avoid asking questions with a choice unless the child really has a choice. Telling a child who is dawdling over his class work 'Do you want to finish the exercise?' suggests to the child with autism that he has choice when in reality he does not.
8. Provide predictability; give adequate information. Let learners know in advance what is going to happen next. Inform them if there is going to be any change in the routine and involve them in making plans. Let them know what is going to happen and what behaviour is expected of them. Giving the child a visual schedule is an excellent way of preparing them for changes and transitions in their daily routine. This could be something as simple as a child's personal daily timetable in addition to the weekly classroom timetable. Tick off activities that have been completed so that what is done and what is yet to come is visually clear.

By following these simple rules you will have established a safe, non-judgmental and empowering space for teaching and learning not just for the child with autism or other disabilities, but also for all children. In the next and concluding section of this chapter, we shall specifically look at a few suggestions that the language teacher in the general classroom can consider and adopt.

Language Comprehension

We have earlier noted that persons with autism, even the highly verbal ones, have difficulties with pragmatics, social conversations and conjecture (Lord and Paul 1997). They also have difficulties with narrative. According to Tager-Flusberg (2004) even persons with autism who develop fluent grammatically correct language can have difficulties with its functional use such as asking for help or asking questions to seek information. Our earlier discussion on the characteristics of autism will help you understand that they have difficulties in constructing and comprehending stories, drawing inferences and imaginative thinking. Vacca (2007) correctly observes that in the elementary classroom, children with autism are frequently excluded from the rich experiences of language learning, particularly creative activities. They find it difficult to decipher passages conveying abstract concepts and respond better to passages that deal with concrete everyday experiences. This is one reason why most do not enjoy fairy tales and fantastical accounts, which are often a staple in primary school. Many compensate for this difficulty by learning entire passages and chapters by rote, without deriving the meaning. Yet language comprehension is an intrinsic part of learning: literature, history, geography, math etc., and this aspect must to be addressed to ensure that it does not impact their overall learning. Here are some examples.

1. Help children develop comprehension skills by making reading meaningful and experiential. Choose or create language comprehension passages about familiar shared routines and interests like getting ready for school, the class picnic, sports day, a festival like holi which possibly all the children participate in.
2. Illustrate story telling/ reading sessions with toy characters. Enact the story or have a child/ children enact the story.
3. Hold sessions on sharing experiences of a class outing or about a class project. Have visual cues available for any child who might need the support.
4. It is observed that since autistic children may have difficulties in imaginative thinking, it is important to teach to their strengths. Ask factual questions like, 'What is happening here? What will happen next?' Use reading materials that talk about practical and authentic experiences rather than fantasy. For example, instructions in a recipe or in the construction of a model are good ways to strengthen comprehension skills (Vacca 2007).
5. Vacca (ibid.) notes that while some autistic children read phonetically, most are natural sight readers. They gain new words by reading labels on household objects, dictionaries and

television captions. While nouns, verbs and prepositions can be taught by using a combination of aids like pictures, gestures, and physical models, teaching the child to comprehend words and situations for which there is no physical referent or representation can be a challenge. The 'wh' words—what, when, where, who—frequently cause problems as the child must understand the context and make inferences to answer these questions. (Siegel 1998 cited in Vacca 2007) Teachers can use pictures for wh-question drills, where wh-questions can be asked. For example, 'Where's the kitty?' or 'What is the girl eating?' or 'Who is standing behind the tree?'

6. Children with autism tend to be visual learners and 'think in pictures'. Make learning visually stimulating with the use of charts, pictures, labels and signs to help children associate the written word with its actual referent.
7. Link learning to the child's interests. If a child is fascinated by cars use examples related to cars and introduce reading materials about cars. This is likely to engage the child's attention and concentration and aid learning. Link the process of reading to projects on favoured topics like trains, cars, animals, planets, food, calendars or television characters. Read-along audio-tapes can help reinforce the learning.

Nothing can replace a sense of achievement. Structure exercises for success so that the learner feels a sense of achievement. Praise the learner often and honestly, and ignore the little things that do not matter.

Conclusion

Across the globe, the number of children receiving diagnoses of autism is on the rise, and India is no exception. While a vast number of these children continue to be confined to a life on the margins of society, there is now far greater awareness of the condition in the public domain. The very fact that this chapter is a part of this book bears testimony to this changing reality. All persons with autism can experience qualitative improvements in their lives with early intervention and appropriate education, whether in special or mainstream classrooms. This chapter primarily addresses language teaching and learning by focusing upon one of the core difficulties that characterise this complex condition. It aims to help teachers reflect upon their own use of language in the classroom setting and its likely outcomes for all children, irrespective of their (dis) ability. It makes a case for an unjudgemental, respectful and enabling classroom environment. It suggests a variety of practical techniques to enable children with autism and their regularly developing peers to develop language comprehension by focusing on their strengths and interests and by helping them understand the nuances of social intercourse that helps them to adjust better to our complex and often confusing world.

References

Action for Autism, New Delhi: *'Communication with People with Autism Reading Material: A Compilation'*.

Jordan, Rita, (1997). *Education of Children and Young People with Autism.* Birmingham University, U. K. Special Needs Education Division of Basic Education, UNESCO

Lord, C., and R. Paul, (1997). 'Language and communication in autism'. In D. Cohen and F. Volkmar (eds), *Handbook of Autism and Pervasive Developmental Disorders*. New York: Wiley, 195–225.

Ministry of Education, Special Programs Branch, British Columbia. (2000). *Teaching students with autism: A resource guide for schools.* http: //www. bced.gov.bc.ca/ specialed/docs/autism.pdf. Last accessed 10 July 2016.

Tager-Flusberg, H., (2004). 'Strategies for conducting research on language in autism'. *Journal of Autism and Developmental Disorders*, 34, 75–8.

Vacca, James S., (2007). 'Autistic children can be taught to read'. *International Journal of Special Education*, 22/ 3, 54–61.

Index